V I E T N A M

AMERICA IN THE WAR YEARS

SERIES EDITOR

David L. Anderson

University of Indianapolis

The Vietnam War and the tumultuous internal upheavals in America that coincided with it marked a watershed era in U.S. history. These events profoundly challenged America's heroic self-image. During the 1950s the United States defined Southeast Asia as an area of vital strategic importance. In the 1960s this view produced a costly American military campaign that continued into the early 1970s. The Vietnam War was the nation's longest war and ended with an unprecedented U.S. failure to achieve its stated objectives. Simultaneous with this frustrating military intervention and the domestic debate that it produced were other tensions created by student activism on campuses, the black struggle for civil rights, and the women's liberation movement. The books in this series explore the complex and controversial issues of the period from the mid-1950s to the mid-1970s in brief and engaging volumes. To facilitate continued and informed debate on these contested subjects, each book examines a military, political, or diplomatic issue; the role of a key individual; or one of the domestic changes in America during the war.

VOLUMES PUBLISHED

Melvin Small. *Antiwarriors: The Vietnam War and the Battle for America's Hearts and Minds* (2002). Cloth ISBN 0-8420-2895-1 Paper ISBN 0-8420-2896-X

Edward K. Spann. *Democracy's Children: The Young Rebels of the 1960s and the Power of Ideals* (2003). Cloth ISBN 0-8420-5140-6 Paper ISBN 0-8420-5141-4

DEMOCRACY'S CHILDREN

DEMOCRACY'S CHILDREN

The Young Rebels of the 1960s and the Power of Ideals

EDWARD K. SPANN

VIETNAM
AMERICA IN THE WAR YEARS
VOLUME 2

A Scholarly Resources Inc. Imprint
Wilmington, Delaware

Scholarly Resources Inc.
104 Greenhill Avenue
Wilmington, DE 19805-1897
www.scholarly.com

Library of Congress Cataloging-in-Publication Data

Spann, Edward K., 1931–
  Democracy's children : the young rebels of the 1960s and the power of ideals /
Edward K. Spann.
     p. cm. — (Vietnam. America in the war years ; v. 2)
  Includes bibliographical references.
  ISBN 0-8420-5140-6 (alk. paper) — ISBN 0-8420-5141-4 (pbk. : alk. paper)
  1. Baby boom generation—United States. 2. United States—Social
conditions—1945– 3. United States—Social conditions—1960–1980.
4. Radicalism—United States. 5. Protest movements—United States.
6. Counterculture—United States. 7. Nineteen sixties. I. Title. II. Series.
HN59 .S668 2004
305.2—dc21
                                                                  2003008944

Acknowledgments

This book, like most broad studies, owes much to the previous work of many other historians, too numerous for all of them to be mentioned. The following have made special contributions to this work: Terry Anderson, Todd Gitlin, Landon Y. Jones, and James Miller. Since my work depends heavily on primary sources, especially contemporary magazine articles, I also owe much to the efforts of helpful librarians, particularly those at Indiana State University.

About the Author

Edward K. Spann, emeritus professor of history and distinguished professor in arts and sciences at Indiana State University, is the author of six previous books: *Ideals and Politics: New York Intellectuals and Nineteenth-Century Liberalism* (1972; nominated for a Pulitzer Prize), *The New Metropolis: New York City* (1981; winner of the Dixon Ryan Fox Award in 1977), *Brotherly Tomorrows: Movements for a Cooperative Society in America* (1989), *Hopedale: From Commune to Company Town* (1992), *Designing Modern America: The Regional Planning Association and Its Members* (1996), and *Gotham at War: New York City, 1860–1865* (2002). He is currently working on a biography of the artist-writer Gilbert Brown Wilson.

Contents

Introduction

In my earlier works on significant aspects of social idealism in nineteenth-
and twentieth-century America, I have dealt with the antigovernment liberalism of the Jacksonian Era; the movement for a cooperative society
that began with New Harmony and culminated in Debsian socialism; a
model religious community based on Christian Non-Resistance at
Hopedale, Massachusetts; and the effort to establish regional planning as
the guiding influence over the development of modern urban America in
the post–World War I era. My aim has been to study such ideals not as
intellectual abstractions but as living articles of faith that have animated
the thought and behavior of significant populations. Studied that way,
each set of ideals reveals much about the problems and promise of its age.

Now, in *Democracy's Children*, my subject is the movement to expand democratic ideals to embrace not only adult white males but also
black Americans and, eventually, women and others, a movement that
brought a radical redefinition of American society. It is my contention
that a portion of the generation born in the 1940s was educated by a
special set of influences to a sense of democratic mission, which they attempted to fulfill when they began to reach maturity in the 1960s. In
some respects, this is the not unfamiliar story of high ideals meeting ob-
durate society, a story with a familiar ending: the disappointment of idealism. But it goes beyond conflict between young idealists and adult society,
for society itself may be said to have created the mission.

In my effort to provide a truthful understanding of this development,
I have rejected some often entertained assumptions that have subtly but
significantly distorted it. One is that the baby boom, which spawned the
"youth revolution" of the 1960s, developed after World War II, whereas
in fact it began in 1940. It was the generation born in the decade of the
1940s that formed the rebel army of political and cultural protest in the
1960s. Related to this fact is some confusion regarding the fundamental
subdivisions within the baby-boom generation. Although there is growing awareness that this generation consisted of what I have long called
two waves, at least one history of the 1960s insists that these were no

more than two branches associated, respectively, with politics and culture, whereas they were actually two generational subsets associated with distinct periods of time. A third common error is that youth in the 1960s were guided by ideas of their own invention—a reflection of some generation gap—whereas in fact these ideas were learned from the older generation. A fourth error is that the 1960s was caused by the inadequacies of the 1950s, a belief that puts the two decades at odds, whereas the 1950s helped mold democracy's children in more positive ways. In sum, this is the story not of some generational conflict but of more complex relationships involving longitudinal differences in American society, which had less to do with age than with class and geographic location.

Democracy's children represented generally urban, middle-class strivings to realize democratic ideals, strivings that produced interesting results in the form of an "equality revolution" that came to embrace an unanticipated spectrum of human differences. This study begins with the birth of democracy's children in the 1940s; it traces their childhood development in the schools and elsewhere to the first stages of maturity and beyond in the 1960s and early 1970s, increasingly tumultuous years when their democratic ideals encountered the seemingly undemocratic authority of universities and governments. Finally, it deals with their reintegration into American society in the 1970s and 1980s, an event with significant if not entirely appreciated implications for the future.

There are numerous elements in this complex story, including child-raising ideals, the "sexual revolution," drugs, sports, music, college education, the New Left, war resistance, black power, feminism, politics, and popular culture. It is hoped that the sum of these elements forms an accurate portrait of a special part of a special generation, a portrait that will add significantly to our understanding of American democratic society in the second half of the twentieth century.

CHAPTER One

GENESIS

THE 1960s WILL PROBABLY ALWAYS BE BEST KNOWN AS THE YEARS OF THE youth rebellion, a period when young idealists seemed ready to transform American society in radical ways. Among the several causes of this phenomenon, the most significant was the character of the young rebels themselves. They were shaped by various influences, but the strongest and most common developed out of the special circumstances associated with their birth in the late 1930s and, especially, the 1940s. In a general sense, they were the product of the World War II era, a time of democratic idealism different from the consumer-oriented, materialistic 1950s that especially shaped the majority of later baby boomers. Education in democratic idealism gave this "forties generation" its special character and direction when it reached maturity in the 1960s.

As the advance guard of the baby boom, the forties generation forced basic changes in American attitudes and institutions at every stage of its development, the result of both its upbringing and its sheer size. Initially, its importance and its size were not recognized. It had long been assumed that an increasingly urban and modern America would experience a sharp drop in the birthrate from its more agricultural days, and indeed, in the 1930s this drop did occur, reinforced by the privations of the Great Depression. At the end of World War II, however, some demographers began to recognize that the decline in the birthrate had at least temporarily been reversed. In 1946, Frank W. Notestein, director of the Office of Population Research at Princeton, pointed out that an increase in the number of babies had begun modestly in the late 1930s and then had shot up during the war years. At the very middle of the war, 1943 was the first year in American history when births exceeded 3 million. By 1945 there were 1 million more children than had been predicted.

Other than sheer quantity, the most striking thing about this development was that it occurred throughout American society, in city as well as countryside, in every section of the country, in every class, and in every race and religion. Although the birthrate did vary from group to group, it is significant that the rate rose for every group and that it rose fastest in those groups that had had the lowest birthrates. The increase was especially great in the urban middle class and greater still among well-educated women. Between 1940 and 1947, whereas there was a 22 percent increase in births for women in general, it was 55 percent for women with one to three years of college education, and 77 percent for those with four or more years of college. "Should this trend continue into the future," said one population expert, "students of differential fertility some day may well be seeking an explanation of a direct rather than inverse relationship between education, occupation, and fertility."[1] Having babies had become a special trend among those men and women who were likely to have the greatest influence on society.

In the 1940s, more than 29 million children were born, increasing the percentage of those under ten years of age from 16 percent of the population in 1940 to close to 20 percent in 1950. This formidable mass of children had an impact on American society at every stage in their growth: as infants, stimulating the production of such things as diapers and baby food; as children, prompting the great migration to the new postwar suburbs and putting great pressure on American schools; as adolescents, creating a youth market suited to their special needs and also threatening a crisis in the social order; as young adults, mounting an unprecedented challenge both to the nation's colleges and to the nation itself.

Besides their sheer numbers, the forties babies grew up under circumstances that often gave them a general character different not only from older people but also from the younger members of the baby boom. If nothing else, they tended to be the oldest children in postwar families and so more exposed to both parental and societal expectations and training than their younger siblings born in the fifties. And they were often exposed to some special values associated with the New Deal and with World War II, notably democratic—sometimes radically democratic—values. It was these new Americans who became what I call democracy's children, a formidable mass of special young people who were to pose a profound challenge to American society in the name of democratic changes that their parents had conceived of but did not realize.

What explained this boom in democratic babies? Undoubtedly, the widespread affluence of the war and postwar years made it possible for many young couples to marry and to begin families at an early age; during the 1940s and 1950s the percentage of unmarried women was cut in half, and the average age of marriage for women decreased from 21.5 to 20 years. Affluence also made larger families possible; the period saw a relative decline of families with only one child in favor of those with three and four children. Various secondary encouragements for families included improvements in infant health care, the desire to escape military conscription, income tax exemptions, and the effects of postwar teacher shortages in persuading school administrators to abandon their prejudice against hiring married women.

Such factors alone, however, cannot explain the procreation mania that swept through every class during these years. Fundamentally, the reason millions of babies were born was simply that millions of men and especially women *wanted* families with an intensity unequaled during any other time in the twentieth century. At the root of it all was an idealism that was both extraordinary and ordinary, the product of special times. World War II was the longest and bloodiest foreign war that the United States had fought and the one that had the greatest effect on its society. Although more than 300,000 Americans died in the conflict, and although it ended under the mushroom cloud of the new nuclear age, it was in many respects the "good war" fought by those who were eventually proclaimed "the greatest generation"—the parents who initiated the baby boom. The war established the United States as the dominant power in the world; it brought the nation out of the Great Depression; and it introduced Americans to the longest period of prosperity in their history.

It was also a great victory for democracy over the totalitarianism that had threatened the world during the previous decade. As such, it gave significant new force and direction to American idealism, much of which survived into the next decades despite the anxieties of the Cold War, the hypocrisies of the McCarthy era, and the complacent materialism of the prosperous years. Whereas World War I had introduced cynicism, World War II introduced hope for a new and better world.

The full extent of this hope was obscured by the fact that most of it was invested in private relations rather than in the public sphere, especially in a new version of the family. At the end of the war, ordinary Americans sought to make their own families the little worlds in which they chose to spend their most essential lives and where they expected to realize most of life's satisfactions. The war itself helped to make marriage and, by extension, family fashionable; the Census Bureau estimated that between 1940 and 1943 there were at least 1 million more weddings than normal, and there was an even greater surge in the immediate postwar period as a flood of GIs returned to civilian life looking to marry—a search shared by American women. By 1951 the percentage of unmarried women in America had fallen from 28 in 1940 to 9—the lowest rate since the recording of marital status began in 1890, when 34 percent of women were not married.

The disruptions of the war period, following as they did the frustrations of the Depression, created a deep need for family. A returning veteran especially looked for "home," that humanized bit of space where he and his wife and children could create their own intimate little world. In Sloan Wilson's best-selling novel *The Man in the Gray Flannel Suit*, the protagonist Tom Rath returns from service in Europe, where he has killed nineteen men, seeking the time to raise a family: "The important thing is to create an island of order in a sea of chaos." When he is offered the chance of a lifetime to achieve the wealth and power of the executive world, he chooses to remain with a nine-to-five job that will assure him time to be with his wife and children.[2]

Tom Rath's thinking was common to the women as well as the men of his time. War propaganda had depicted the conflict as a struggle to return the lunatic world to a gentler era of friends and families. Women defense workers were encouraged to believe that their work would help make the world safe for the homes to which both they and their men would return at war's end. "The women want their men to come home," declared *Time* magazine in 1945. "With a unanimity which would startle old time feminists they want to quit jobs, settle down and have children. Three years of war, much of it spent in furnished rooms or with in-laws or in trailers or small hotels, has put a lovely light around the little white cottage."[3] In the unstable and anxious world that grew up around Americans in the postwar years, the family acquired a new appeal as a secure haven where it would be possible for ordinary people to live life as they wanted to live it.

The immediate postwar years brought a challenge to the developing family ideal, for many hasty wartime marriages fell apart. In 1946, when there were 613,000 divorces, the divorce rate reached an all-time high of

17.8 per thousand, more than double the 1940 rate, leading one authority to warn that unless the trend were modified, there would soon be one divorce for every two marriages. Concern over the divorce rate continued well into the 1950s, but by then it was apparent that the institution of marriage had survived the postwar storm. In 1957, one writer was able to declare that "divorce is going out of style," noting that the divorce rate had declined to half that of 1946 and was still falling.[4]

The fact was that Americans, although they had the highest divorce rate in the world, were also extraordinarily devoted to family life. Margaret Mead, the anthropologist, observed that as a generally gregarious people little practiced in self-sufficient isolation, they had a special need for familial companionship. Although the hunger for normality and family contributed to the upsurge of postwar divorces, in that anticipation easily outran reality, the great majority of the separated soon found new partners and more stable marriages. The postwar concern over divorce mobilized powerful influences in support of the family. In 1945, Mead had warned that the war had disrupted the routines on which family life had been based in the past, and she called for a public effort to reestablish the family: "It will take a concerted effort, for those who live in it and those who live by writing about it, to restyle it so that it is livable for those human beings who are caught between one family form and another."[5]

Some advocates of the renewed family proposed the creation of public family-support services such as nurseries for the children of working women, but little was accomplished along this line except for the spread of family-life education programs connected with the schools. More important was a partly spontaneous campaign to strengthen the devotion of individuals to the family ideal, a conservative response that required some resolution of a radical problem. As virtually all agreed, the war had accelerated the decline of the traditional family and of the gender roles on which it was based. Strengthening the family against changing times, then, required a new delineation of gender roles suited to contemporary conditions—especially of the role of women, which had been altered not only by the long-term influence of feminism but also by the new opportunities afforded by the war. With the departure of millions of men to the battlefields, jobs once monopolized by men were opened to women, inspiring hopes for a time when females would have equal opportunities with males to pursue their ambitions outside the home. Although, with demobilization, millions of women gave up these jobs voluntarily or otherwise, the fact remained that the war had drawn them away from their traditional roles.

Much of the effort to define woman's role was made by antifeminists, most notably by several college-educated women. Among the leading influences in that effort was Marynia Farnham, a psychiatrist and coauthor of the influential book *Modern Women: The Lost Sex* (1947). Farnham lashed out at feminists for urging women to seek careers in conflict with men and in contradiction to what she proclaimed their own natures and needs to be. What women needed was to be restored to their roles as wives and mothers, to a situation that would meet their natural "wish for dependence, inwardness, a wish to be protected and made secure, a strong desire for passivity and compliance."[6]

Another antifeminist, Agnes E. Meyer, a mother and also a trustee of Barnard College, urged women to recognize that although they might have many careers, they had "only one vocation—motherhood." Meyer called on women to play their part in restoring "security in our insecure world" by committing their talents to establishing a strong and sound family life. Other advocates of the New Domesticity also emphasized the essential importance of woman's role in the home. For women who felt uncomfortable in identifying themselves simply as housewives, the author Dorothy Thompson advised that this role was actually a complex and important one as business manager, teacher, and more generally a determining influence on the future of society: "The homemaker, the nurturer, the creator of childhood's environment, is the constant creator of culture, civilization and virtue."[7]

The New Domesticity had taken hold among well-educated, middle-class women by the end of the 1940s. Betty Friedan, who would later tag that outlook "the feminine mystique," remembered that in 1949 "domestic bliss had suddenly become chic." For Friedan, family became a substitute not only for the career in psychology for which she had been preparing but also for the liberal politics that had drawn her into the short-lived Progressive Party in 1948. The family "was a comfortable little world you could really do something about," and "at home, you were necessary, you were important, you were the boss."[8] Other women also believed that they had found their true importance in the home. Being female had some definite advantages, said one author in the *Woman's Home Companion*, particularly since in her job as a housewife she was essentially her own boss, setting most of the rules for her family to follow. The fact that the proponents of the domestic role often enjoyed the special benefits of advantaged social position seems not to have diminished their ability to convince many other women less blessed that marriage and family were their natural destiny.

The New Domesticity was not a resurrection of the old patriarchal household, however, for the postwar world brought no definition of man's role as sure as that for woman. The result was to weaken traditional gender distinctions. "Literature in the United States," said Margaret Mead in 1948, "is rancorous and angry on the whole question of the relationship between men and women. We have had a spate of books that claim that women are being masculinized . . . and another spate . . . that insist that men are being feminized."[9] In comic strips, on radio, and later on television, men were often caricatured as bumbling, henpecked husbands strikingly different from the he-men of earlier days.

What appeared to be weakness by patriarchal standards, however, was often an adjustment of men to new circumstances. For many, the times had demolished the idea that the male was the sole breadwinner. When asked in 1945 whether they thought girls should plan for careers other than homemaking, 55 percent of boys in the poll answered "yes," and only 23 percent said "no." Although "Rosie the Riveter" disappeared at the end of the war, a great many women continued to hold jobs, including many married women. Between 1940 and 1950 the number of working wives nearly doubled; this wage-earning employment made possible many of the early marriages common to the period.

As the economic basis for male dominance was weakening, its moral basis, too, was questioned by postwar ideology. The war against totalitarianism had left little room for any kind of autocratic rule, discouraging the ideal of male domination in favor of a democratic ideal of marriage as a partnership of relative equals. On the physical level the ideal often included the expectation that women as well as men would find sexual satisfaction in the marital relationship. More generally, it meant that wives would have an important voice in family decisions and also that men would assume a share of the day-to-day responsibilities of family living. The democratic ideal was hardly all-pervasive—even democratically disposed men rarely accepted an equal share of dirty diapers and dusty corners—but it did encourage men to take a stronger role than their fathers in the whole business of nurturing their young, to serve as partners with their wives in maintaining the family as a place for joint satisfaction.

Beyond the old reasons of food and sex, men and women were motivated to marry by a common ideal of family as a joint personal and private enterprise for life. If in the larger world of power politics and Cold War diplomacy the individual counted for very little, in the family he and she could build a life and a future particularly their own. Generally, the key to that enterprise was parenthood and several children. This attitude was both reflected in and reinforced by the advertising of the period. One advertisement for 7-Up, for instance, featured a picture of a happy family of five (father, mother, son, daughter, and baby) with the mother playing a piano, the father strumming a ukulele, and the son blowing into a saxophone: "Be a 'Fresh-Up Family.' It's fun when the whole family gathers around Mom at the piano." Little wonder that the times brought the coinage, probably by *McCall's* magazine, of the term "togetherness" to describe the dominant family ideal.[10]

In the past, even with a limited range of birth-control techniques, the better-educated had succeeded in controlling the size of their families. Especially during the Depression, most preferred no more than two children. In the 1940s, though, they upped the limit to three or four and more. In 1948, for instance, one survey of eighteen- to twenty-five-year-olds found that 60 percent of those who had some college education favored three to four children, versus 44 percent among those with only a grammar-school education. Why? Among several reasons, the most general seems to have been that, as one father said, "There is a certain security in numbers." That security was psychological rather than economic: children had value not as workers but as citizens of the little family worlds over which parents would preside. Although families were economically dependent on the larger world, ideally they could be emotionally independent, their homes the places where love, joy, and satisfaction could be assured regardless of the times. "Wars can come, jobs can go, money can run out," proclaimed one author in 1951, "but if father, mother, and children stand by each other, hope and happiness may survive."[11]

Critics eventually came to view the New Domesticity as a selfish retreat from a problem-ridden world in the search for a false security. "The explanation for large families," wrote one critic in 1961, "apparently lies in some notion that the world is cold, lonely, and dangerous, and children will make it less so or shield us from it. It is a strange notion for such a practical generation in a dangerous world."[12] This naysaying reflected a repudiation of what sociologists called antisocial "privatism," a repudiation that was to have a significant influence on the thinking of the 1960s.

Postwar parents, however, saw the private family world as something they had earned by years of enforced involvement in forces beyond their control. Wartime propaganda had encouraged the idea that they were engaged in a struggle to preserve a way of life of which the family was the most vital part. Although they expected to reap great emotional benefits from family life, they could also believe that they were participating in society at its most fundamental level. The children they raised were extensions of themselves, to be prepared for new and better attainments as participants in a better future. They listened to Harry Emerson Fosdick, a popular philosopher of the time, when he placed the home at the top of the "vital groups" which, more than nations, ultimately shaped the nature of society; it was in such intimate groups "where the leaven of decency, kindness, good will, and love has got its start."[13] Through their efforts, parents could bequeath to the future progeny who would not only achieve individual success but also make a respectable contribution to the welfare of society.

Well-educated parents especially accepted a responsibility to prepare their children for a constructive role in a democratic world. The war against totalitarianism had given new importance to the ideal of the democratic family. One study conducted in the late 1950s of the attitude of Vassar graduates indicated that the women in the classes of 1940 to 1943 were the most emphatic in rejecting the idea that "obedience and respect for authority are the most important virtues that children should learn."[14] Rather, for many educated mothers of this generation, the aim was to teach democratic habits and values. In 1946, Mildred Welsh Cranston, the wife of a Dartmouth College professor, urged women to give special attention to educating the next generation for peace in the world by teaching them to reject class snobbishness and especially racial prejudice, undemocratic attitudes that bred conflict.

Parents were told that for children to learn democracy, they must be treated in a democratic way. In 1950 the Midcentury White House Conference on Children and Youth—the first national conference on children to be held in a decade—published a lengthy "Pledge to Children," which included the promise that "we will work to rid ourselves of prejudice and discrimination, so that together we may achieve a truly democratic society." The authors of the pledge believed that there could be no genuine democracy unless children were educated to accept the worth and dignity of every person, beginning with the dignity of the children themselves. Democracy also required the inclusion of children in family and community decisions affecting them—an ideal which the Midcentury Conference incorporated in its own planning committees, where young people were to "be accepted as full equals in all aspects of the conference work."[15]

Various observers had noted a trend in the 1940s toward the democratic family. In 1950 the prominent psychologist Erik Erickson said that the typical American family "harbors more democracy than meets the eye" and that it furnished a key to understanding the nature and direction of the democratic process. He made special note of the disposition within the family to protect the rights of every member, a concern for the individual that mandated a general policy of consensus in decision-making. Erickson commended this rejection of aristocracy and inequality but also noted something less positive, a tendency to diminish the place of emotions among family members: "Both overt loving and overt hating are kept on a low key, for either might weaken the balance of the family."[16] Most likely, this tendency helped set the stage for the explosive search for emotional freedom in the 1960s.

Neither the positive nor negative attributes of the democratic family were especially new; Alexis de Tocqueville had seen them in the American family a century earlier. The postwar family, however, was subject to a relatively new influence that both enriched and complicated its chararacter: the influence of psychology. With the popularization of Freudianism, Americans of the 1940s and 1950s experienced a psychological revolution that affected their views of human nature. By the 1960s the greater part of the reading public was at least vaguely familiar with such Freudian concepts as the Oedipus complex, sublimation, frustration, and inferiority feelings. However ready they were to adopt Freudian ideas, though, many Americans were not satisfied by Sigmund Freud's fundamental pessimism regarding human nature and chose the more optimistic humanistic psychology of Carl Rogers and Abraham Maslow, which offered the hope that the individual self had a vast and as yet unrealized potential for virtue and happiness. But whatever the particular school, the popularization of psychology encouraged people to look for psychological explanations for behavior—sometimes overdoing it. "If Johnny throws a spitball at Mary, nothing so ordinary as mischief is afoot," one observer complained. "The possibilities have to be—are joyously—entertained that Johnny is working off aggression, compensating for deeply felt inferiority, asserting his masculinity."[17]

The psychological revolution gave a new importance to parenthood. If the traditional parent had the primary responsibility for the moral character of his offspring, the modern parent had the more complex task of guiding the psychological development of her children during the long period of their emotional dependency. Informed and sensitive parents could raise a new generation free from the debilitating inhibitions and frustrations that had afflicted humankind; under the guidance of experts, they could create personalities emotionally healthier than themselves, capable of achieving higher levels of happiness and self-satisfaction. Conversely, though, ignorant and uncaring parents could distort the personalities of their offspring—a proposition that yielded the cliché, "There are no problem children, only problem parents." George J. Hecht, publisher of *Parents Magazine*, said that "institutions filled to overflowing with mentally disturbed men and women and young people are horrifying proof" of the failure of parents to understand their children's emotional needs.[18] In general, psychology imposed on the family responsibilities and goals that were bound to create disillusionment and guilt.

The work of democratic parenting was further complicated by a change of emphasis in child-rearing philosophy from discipline to permissiveness. Earlier child-care guides had urged parents to follow a strict regimen in the feeding and toilet training of their infants. The baby "should learn that hunger will be satisfied only so often," wrote one expert in 1929. "He will begin to learn that he is part of a world bigger than his own desires." The restrictive approach remained alive in the 1940s, but the new permissive philosophy was gaining ground, and the emphasis shifted from preparing the child for a place in the world to allowing maximum freedom for the development of his own basic nature. The aim earlier had been to establish control over the badness in a baby's nature; now it was to remove unreasonable restraints on her natural growth. "Babies are born deeply conditioned toward love and cooperation and self-development," wrote two experts in 1953. "It is only when they meet resistance to their own inner needs that so-called 'badness' develops."[19]

The new doctrine conformed to the ideal of the democratic family. It emphasized respect for each infant as a unique individual, and it rejected the autocratic idea that parents always knew what was best for the child. Where once the remote and punishing patriarch had occupied his throne, now there stood the accommodating democratic father eager to form a loving relationship with his children and to treat them democratically. If the child was not king, at least he was an equal. Ideally, this family egalitarianism promised to nurture not only healthier personalities but also more democratic attitudes. In 1948 a study of racial and ethnic prejudices in children yielded the conclusion that children raised in democratic families were oriented more toward love and were more likely to judge others on the basis of intrinsic worth rather than race or nationality. The 1960s were to provide support for this claim.

These child-oriented doctrines often found support in public education, the first world into which the young graduated from the family.

Here, too, was great promise mixed with uncertainty, particularly in the 1950s, which saw a sharp change in both educational philosophy and aims.

The overall result was to make the forties generation the best-educated generation in American history—and also one of the most disquieted.

NOTES

1. Charles F. Westoff, "Differential Fertility in the United States, 1900–1952," *American Sociological Review* 19 (1954): 551, 555, 561.

2. Sloan Wilson, *The Man in the Gray Flannel Suit* (New York, 1955), 109, 182.

3. Quoted in Richard R. Lingerman, *Don't You Know There's a War On* (New York, 1970), 96.

4. Albert Q. Maisel, "Divorce Is Going Out of Style," *Reader's Digest* (August 1955): 35.

5. Margaret Mead, "What's the Matter with the Family," *Harper's Magazine* 190 (1944–45): 398.

6. Marynia F. Farnham, "Battles Won and Lost," *Annals of the American Academy of Political and Social Sciences* 251 (1947): 113–19; and idem, "Helping Boys to Be Boys, Girls to Be Girls," *Parents Magazine* 28 (January 1952): 34–35.

7. Agnes E. Meyer, "Women Aren't Men," *Atlantic Monthly* 186 (August 1948): 32–36; Dorothy Thompson, "Occupation—Housewife," *Reader's Digest* (May 1949): 25–26.

8. Betty Friedan, *It Changed My Life* (New York, 1976), 8–16.

9. Margaret Mead, *Male and Female* (New York, 1949), 300.

10. *Parents Magazine* 26 (October–November 1950): 27; Hugh R. King, "E Pluribus Togetherness," *Harper's Magazine* 215 (August 1952): 51–53.

11. Henry C. Link, "Love, Marriage—and Security," *Reader's Digest* (May 1951): 47.

12. Nora Johnson, "The Captivity of Marriage," *Atlantic Monthly* 207 (1961): 41.

13. Harry Emerson Fosdick, "A Faith for Tough Times," *Reader's Digest* (December 1952): 87–88.

14. Marvin B. Freedman, "Changes in Six Decades of Some Attitudes and Values Held by Educated Women," *Journal of Social Issues* 17, no. 1 (1961): 25–26.

15. Midcentury White House Conference on Children and Youth, *Proceedings* (Raleigh, NC, 1951), 28–29, 32, 37, 250.

16. Erik H. Erickson, *Childhood and Society*, 2d ed. (New York, 1958), 316–18.

17. Catherine MacKenzie, "What Is Spoiling?" *New York Times* (September 5, 1948): 27; John R. Seeley, "The Americanization of the Unconsciousness," *Atlantic Monthly* 208 (1961): 70–72.

18. George J. Hecht, "Urge Passage of the National Child Research Bill," *Parents Magazine* 24 (April 1949): 18.

19. Sophia L. Fahs and Constance J. Fostex, "Character: The Key to a Good Life," *Parents Magazine* 28 (April 1953): 82.

CHAPTER Two

SCHOOLING IN CHANGING TIMES

A T THE TIME THAT THE FORTIES GENERATION ENTERED IT, THE nation's school system was undergoing a longtime educational revolution that was to continue throughout their formative years. During most of the 1940s there had been a decline in school population as a result of earlier low birthrates, but before the end of the decade the first enrollments of forties babies reversed this trend and by 1955 the increase in enrollments for each year had grown so large that it equaled the entire increase for the two decades before 1950. The postwar school system was ill prepared to meet this demand. Society was slow to recognize the implications of the baby boom, but by 1949 the alarm was raised. Writing in the *Saturday Evening Post*, Henry and Katharine Pringle noted that the 7 million births predicted for the years 1941 to 1946 had actually turned out to be 17 million, and they warned that Americans confronted a major school crisis: "Badly paid teachers are quitting the elementary grades in unprecedented numbers. High schools do not exist in many rural areas and are overcrowded everywhere. Equality of opportunity for brains . . . seems to be a gradually vanishing ideal."[1] In 1952 the Federal Security Administration estimated that 60 percent of the nation's classrooms were overcrowded.

Typically, the nation was slow to face the problem but eventually strong in its achievements. In "An Open Letter to Parents" (1949), Dwight D.

Eisenhower, then president of Columbia University, urged parents to join with teachers in a "community partnership" for educational improvement. Overall, the crisis activated a powerful lobby of professional educators and laymen in support of better schools, much of the work being done by various citizens' committees with the support of the Parent-Teacher Association (whose membership more than doubled, to 5 million members, during the 1940s). As a result, public spending for the schools rose from $439 per pupil in 1946 to $596 in 1950 and, after a decade of much-expanded enrollment, to $766 in 1960; as a percentage of the gross national product, spending increased from 1.4 percent in 1946 to 3.1 percent in 1960. By 1960 the United States had succeeded in providing space in its public schools for nearly 11 million more students than there had been in 1950, the biggest increase in its history.

These physical accomplishments had greater benefit for those students born in the 1950s than for those born during the previous decade. The first wave of baby boomers were the ones most exposed both to the shortages and to the public response to them. In other respects, too, the members of the forties generation were influenced by conditions different from those that affected both their older and younger cohorts. They came of school age, for instance, during an especially intense phase of the Cold War, when the rapid progress made by the Soviet Union in the development of nuclear weapons shattered the sense of security that Americans had enjoyed during their brief monopoly of nuclear power after World War II. And during the early 1950s the United States became engrossed in the Korean War, which threatened to become a larger conflict with Communist China as well as the Soviet Union. Inevitably, some of these tensions penetrated the child's world, although probably less than many observers believed. At school, pupils were drilled to drop to the floor under their desks to "protect" themselves from bombs.

Other tensions involved public concern over the supposed influence of communism in the public schools, an often irrational worry that led the nation's largest patriotic organization, the American Legion, to accuse the largest educational organization, the National Education Association, of "un-American" tendencies. Socially active teachers ran the risk, complained an educator in 1950, of being denounced by superpatriots as traitors. Eric Hodgins, in his period novel, *Blanding's Way*, had his hero refuse to support openly a hot-lunch program for his daughter's school on the grounds that it was sure to be denounced as Communist inspired: "The hot lunch is part of the cold war."[2] Scarsdale, New York, was driven by demands that the "subversive" novels of Howard Fast be purged from its libraries. The effect of such incidents was mixed. At one extreme, the focus on the red menace helped some parents to instill the values of super-patriotism in their own children. At the other, resistance to the anti-red panic by more liberal-minded parents served to instill a respect for freedom of opinion and a contempt for mindless patriotism in their progeny. The development of a kind of anti-anti-red attitude was to become a powerful influence in the 1960s.

Despite the drama of these conflicts, however, most schoolchildren were more significantly influenced by their daily exposure to the school system devised for them. Especially notable was the emphasis on democracy as an educational objective in the postwar era. The function of the schools in promoting American democracy was almost as old as the Republic, but it acquired special strength in the 1940s when the United States first vanquished a totalitarianism of the right, only to encounter a totalitarianism of the left. Democracy, wrote one educator, was the governing principle that "must determine the whole practical operation of education, in all aspects, large and small, right down to details."[3]

Although most Americans agreed on the importance of such a mission, they often disagreed over how to fulfill it. Many believed that public education should indoctrinate the young into the American Way, teaching reverence for the symbols as well as the principles of national life. Especially for patriotic organizations such as the American Legion, the school was an important weapon in the domestic as well as foreign war against communism. An influential minority of liberal-minded parents, however, believed that even the best-intended indoctrination was authoritarian and so inimical to true democracy; children needed to experience freedom in their own school lives if they were to develop a full understanding of the democratic way.

These basic differences often came to a focus in the great debate over what was generally called "progressive" (or "new" or "modern") education. The progressive approach found some of its strongest support among those who also believed in democratic parenting. Its essential character involved what one of its proponents called a "vigorous commitment to radical democratic means and radically democratic ends."[4] It placed the student at the center of the school, establishing the child's primary importance. Teachers were not to attempt to impose a uniform learning on all the young; rather, they were to provide the individual child only with what his development had prepared him to receive. This respect for the individuality of the learner was linked with a rejection of the importance of subject matter and of the teacher's own experience as an adult. The rapid advances in modern knowledge, so it was said, quickly rendered established learnings obsolete; therefore, the schools should concentrate on developing in children the skills and attitudes that would enable them to acquire what would be worth knowing in the future. In this view, the child was potentially wiser than the teacher, and preparation for the future was more valuable than knowledge derived from the past.

Progressive education also raised pleasing visions of miniature democracies in which children would make the decisions affecting their school life, thus learning active and responsible participation in their collective sphere as well as the subject matter that interested them. The Citizen Education Project, widely adopted by high schools in the early 1950s, reflected a common hope of teaching "youngsters to become active, informed, alert citizens in the same way they are taught to be good chemists—by laboratory practice."[5] After years of such experience, young Americans would emerge from the schools equipped with habits and skills in democratic living far beyond those possessed by their parents.

Progressivism also encouraged some extravagant and even utopian expectations that the schools could be used to work a radical improvement in society. If society did not accommodate the new democratic personality, then it was society that must change. The most extreme form of this thinking was "reconstructionism," the effort of two New York professors of education, George S. Counts and Theodore Brameld, to incorporate the radical liberal democracy of the New Deal period into public education. Both men believed that the schools could and should be used to reconstruct the social order along radical democratic lines, particularly by inculcating cooperative habits and attitudes in the young. Although the nature of their new democratic order was often vague, it was plainly oriented toward public economic control and international cooperation in the belief that humankind was becoming increasingly interdependent.

Counts and Brameld believed that the schools should preach the essential equality of all persons and the essential evil of what Brameld called "economic discrimination and patterns of prejudice." In 1950, Brameld dreamed that education would help bring into being a new international order "in which all nationalities, races, and religions receive equal rights in democratic control; an order in which 'world citizenship' thus assumes at least equal status with national citizenship." To foster sexual equality, said Counts, "persisting vestiges of the patriarchal tradition should be removed from the relations of boys and girls." More broadly, all children "should learn together the story of the endless struggle to destroy the barriers of class and caste," with the special goal of eliminating prejudice and discrimination against black Americans. In general, education was to be reconstructed to become, as Brameld phrased it, "a penetrating critic, dynamic leader, and imaginative re-creator" which would help save the modern world from its darker self.[6]

Many of these ideas of the postwar decade reappeared among the rebellious and radical young adults of the 1960s, especially the rejection of authority in the name of individual dignity and equality, the emphasis on creativity and relevance over objective truth, and the tendency to treat the educational system as an instrument of social reconstruction. At least a significant minority of those born in the 1940s were exposed to this influence. Although traditional education continued to dominate in the South and in rural areas, progressivism had a strong influence in city and suburban schools, which graduated a disproportionate number of college-bound students, from which the majority of democracy's children came. If nothing else, it tended to confirm the practices and attitudes that children of democratic parents were learning in their own families.

As they proceeded up the educational ladder toward high school, however, the forties generation encountered increasingly stormy times, often involving a mounting controversy over progressive doctrines and practices. The early 1950s brought a spate of books with such titles as *Quackery in the Public Schools* (by Albert Lynd), *Educational Wastelands* (Arthur Bestor), and *The Diminished Mind* (Mortimer Smith), generally the attacks of laymen against what was presumed to be the progressive educational establishment. Justly or not, progressivism became the whipping boy for a public disturbed and angry over various presumed failings of the public schools. Some people treated its sometimes addleheaded idealism as a sign that the red menace was attempting to capture the mind of American youth. More people condemned it for failing to teach basic skills, instill values, and discipline the mind. And the late 1950s brought new criticisms, especially of what many believed was the intellectual flabbiness of the high schools.

By then, the first members of the forties generation were nearing graduation, a growing proportion destined to move on to higher education. The word was out that college had become the chief doorway to success in modern society, and many parents were becoming concerned with their children's preparation for an educational world that, in its devotion to academic discipline, had been notably resistant to progressivism. Their concern was deepened by various experts who emphasized the growing need for advanced skills and knowledge. Of special significance was the inclusion of women in these thoughts. "If your eye is on a career," wrote a high school counselor in 1958, "you're lucky to be a girl. Never before in history have there been so many job opportunities for women."[7] College-educated women could find positions not only in the traditional areas of teaching and nursing but in such "masculine" fields as science and engineering. And the chances for women to go to college were expanded by the decision of democratic parents to treat their children equally, regardless of gender.

The importance of intellectual skills and understanding for both sexes received a powerful emphasis from a new phase in the Cold War. The fight against the red menace during the McCarthy years had fostered caution and conformity in the schools, but the decade also brought a growing concern over the apparent success of the Soviet Union in training masses of scientists and engineers to challenge American technological superiority. After observing Russian schools in early 1956, George J. Hecht warned in *Parents Magazine* that a combination of longer school terms, attention to the basics, and stress on science and engineering was enabling the Soviets to pull ahead in the "brains race," which he saw as replacing the old emphasis on military brawn: "I came home feeling very much concerned about our apparent debasement of the intellectual."[8] The next year, Hecht's concern became a national obsession when the Soviet Union launched the world's first space satellite. Sputnik shattered the complacent belief that Americans would always be first in technology and ignited a widespread effort to resolve what seemed to be a major educational crisis.

The most immediate impact was on the high school curriculum, where a long decline in the importance of mathematics, science, and foreign languages was partly reversed. Less than a year after Sputnik, Congress passed the National Defense Education Act, providing federal money to strengthen the teaching of these subjects and reflecting an even broader trend toward emphasis on courses with intellectual substance. The new watchwords "excellence" and "competition" replaced "cooperation" and "adjustment." In order to develop "the nation's brain power to its highest potential," said Admiral Hyman G. Rickover, the schools had to establish special programs to train *talented* students: "Anti-intellectualism has long been our besetting sin. With us, hostility to superior intelligence masquerades as belief in the equality of man."[9] For the many studious young people who had been dismissed as "squares" by their peers, the campaign for intellectual excellence created a more favorable climate in which to develop their special talents. This encouragement, combined with the new academic courses established in the schools and the growing pressure to prepare for college, made college-bound high school graduates perhaps the best-educated general group in American history.

The often heavy-handed efforts to mobilize the brain power of young Americans, however, also brought a resurgence of educational progressivism. "Education must deal with the whole person," wrote one progressive in 1958. "It is disconcerting to hear statements to the effect that the main business of the schools is the student's mind. To consider the student's mind as divorced from his emotional and physical state is one of the most dangerous concepts ever introduced into the philosophy of education."[10] Other educators also protested that the emphasis on intellectual excellence threatened to produce a depersonalized system of education that ignored the distinctive needs and characteristics of students as individuals. In 1960, progressivism received a powerful boost from Paul Goodman's *Growing Up Absurd*, a book of special significance to the baby-boom generation particularly in its warnings that the "System" was using education to control the minds of the young.

What did the forties youth themselves think? Although they were still too young to have much access to a public platform, they were reaching an age when at least some of them could publish their thoughts. In 1958, for instance, *Senior Scholastic*, a magazine intended for advanced high school students, called on its readers to express their views regarding the campaign for excellence in education. In the dozen replies that it published, most supported the effort, including two that favored removing uninterested or "slow" students from academic classrooms so that they would not get in the way of the more talented. A few students, however, rejected outright the emphasis on excellence on the grounds that it threatened the American commitment to educate all the young for a democratic life. Before plunging into a crash program of science and technical subjects, said one student, the schools should consider the importance of those courses where "the student is encouraged to form his own conclusions."[11]

These few replies illustrate, if nothing else, the diversity of opinion among the young. Although the great majority allowed themselves to be carried along by the changing currents, many responded in a more active way. Especially for those students whose liberal-democratic backgrounds had given them a strong disposition toward progressive education and its values, the conservative changes of the 1950s were often uncomfortable ones. Certainly, the behavior of many of them in the 1960s indicated that they were not happy with a system that emphasized standards over individual needs and interests; thus, the best-educated youth in American history helped launch an attack on the system that had educated them. In the late 1950s, however, their attitudes were obscured by a larger picture of discontent and concern that marked the coming of age of their entire generation and that extended far beyond the walls of the school.

NOTES

1. Henry F. Pringle and Katharine Pringle, "What about Federal Aid for Schools?" *Saturday Evening Post* (April 16, 1949); and Pringle and Pringle, "Are We Letting Our Children Down? *Saturday Evening Post* (May 13, 1950): 25.

2. Eric Hodgins, *Blanding's Way* (New York, 1950), 186.

3. James L. Mursell, *Principles of Democratic Education* (New York, 1955), 3.

4. William W. Brickman, "The Elementary School," *School and Society* 74 (1951): 422–28; Ernest O. Melby, "Safeguarding America's Freedom through Education," *School and Society* 80 (1954): 193–96.

5. Elizabeth Fagg, "Bold New Programs in Our Schools," *Reader's Digest* (August 1953): 96–97.

6. Theodore Brameld, *Philosophies of Education* (New York, 1955), 152–61, 190–91, 194; George S. Counts, *Education and American Civilization* (New York, 1952), 327–42.

7. *Senior Scholastic* (February 21, 1958): 5–7, 27.

8. George J. Hecht, "The Coming International Brains Race," *Parents Magazine* (November 1956): 35, 74–83.

9. H. G. Rickover, "Let's Stop Wasting Our Greatest Resource," *Saturday Evening Post* (March 2, 1957): 19, 108–11.

10. Norman Harvester, "A Further Case for Progressive Education," *School and Society* 86 (1958): 311–13.

11. *Senior Scholastic* (February 7, 1958): 5; (February 14, 1958): 5; (March 21, 1958): 5; (April 11, 1958): 4; (April 18, 1958): 5.

CHAPTER Three

RESTLESS YOUTH

T HE "CHILDREN'S DECADE" OF THE 1950s PARTLY FULFILLED EX-
pectations. Although school boards were rarely able to provide
enough classrooms and teachers for the ever growing numbers of
young people, the nation could justly claim that it had expanded opportunities for education on the secondary as well as the primary level; in
many schools the quality of education had perhaps never been better and
the diversity of subjects never greater. Elsewhere, too, adults had reason
to be pleased with their provisions for the young. "Our children live in
better homes," declared the North Carolina Committee for Children and
Youth in 1960, "attend better schools, are transported in safer buses, eat
more nutritious meals, travel on better highways, have better health care,
study, play, and live under better supervision, and enjoy more and better
services designed to meet their special needs than they did 10 years ago."[1]
If adults thought they had created a paradise for the young, however, it
was in reality an increasingly troubled paradise for all concerned.

By the end of the 1950s the world of family togetherness was coming
apart, the victim both of its own inadequacies and of numerous social
forces. Probably the most important factor was the arrival of the bulk of
the forties generation at what was for them the strange new world of
adolescence. The years that began with puberty were deeply disturbing
for all concerned. Sloan Wilson's fictitious *Man in the Gray Flannel Suit*

described the experience of real parents: "When the kids were younger we hugged, snuggled and kissed a lot, and I could still feel the warmth of them in my arms, but once they reached their teens they seemed to shrink away from my touch." Where there had been lovable little citizens of the family world, there now appeared awkward, sullen strangers. "Normal healthy adolescents are," wrote one expert, "by adult standards, notably psychopathic, manic, and schizoid in their psychological makeup and behavior."[2]

Most observers took some comfort in the thought that adolescence, a mere transition from childhood to adulthood, would eventually be completed. Adolescents were still dependent children striving for the personhood of men and women they would ultimately attain. The many parents exposed to the developmental outlook of Benjamin Spock and others could hope that their ugly ducklings would soon naturally outgrow the obnoxious stage. The eventual maturity of most adolescents confirmed this commonsense view, but by the late 1950s it was evident that there were unexpected complications in the transitional character of adolescence.

By then it was commonplace that modern society had so lengthened the adolescent period that it had become a distinct phase of human existence. Because of improved nutrition and better health, children were growing bigger and faster than ever before, advancing into puberty as much as a year or more earlier than their parents' generation. Moreover, as they matured more rapidly physically, the combination of democratic child-rearing practices, parental social pressures, and exposure to the mass media also made them more sophisticated than ever before. At its other end, though, the period of adolescent dependency had already been extended into the late teens by prohibitions against child labor and the lengthened period of public education. And of special importance for the forties generation, the children of the middle class faced an even longer dependency because of growing expectations that they would go on to college.

This near-decade of adolescence seemed necessary to prepare youth for a constructive role in modern society, but it had significant if not severe costs. After what had generally been the undemanding years of childhood, teenagers in middle-class families began to encounter the full force of parental expectations that they prepare themselves for a successful career, diminishing the opportunities to experience "real" life which the less advantaged seemed to have. These expectations came at a time when the young had begun to hunger for a life of their own. "When sexual desires are more powerful than they will ever be again," observed a sociologist in

1961, "sexual opportunities are fewest; obedience and submission are asked of adolescents at precisely the time when their strength, energy, and desire for autonomy are ascendant."[3] Little wonder that many teens grew silent and secretive if not outright rebellious during the long passage out of childhood.

The trouble was both moderated and intensified by the special world that adolescents created for themselves, generally with the acquiescence and often the approval of their parents. Set apart from the family and from the classroom, this world centered on the peer group, a miniature society of the like-minded and the like-troubled where some freedom from parents and other adults was assured. Although it exerted its own pressures to conform, the peer group at least allowed its members some space to develop their own personal identities. Previous generations of teenagers had often focused their lives on friendships within their own age group, but several features of the 1950s dramatically enlarged the influence of this teen society. One factor was the sheer power of numbers. By 1955, when the 3 million children born in 1943 were approaching puberty, there were more than 15 million teenagers, with even greater numbers soon to follow. Moreover, this large age group was unusually free and unusually well heeled. Although the combination of child-labor laws and general affluence meant that few teenagers worked full time, many enjoyed some income from allowances or part-time jobs. In 1959 a market researcher estimated that teenagers had four times as much money to spend as those in 1945 had had, giving them a total purchasing power of $9.5 billion and making them a powerful consumer group. Among the first adults to discover the so-called generation gap were businessmen eager to develop and exploit the teenage market. The fact that the money was discretionary —uncommitted except as it was directed by teenage fashions—invited attention to teenagers as a distinct group.

The sense of teen importance and difference was reinforced by several magazines established in the 1950s. Various youth magazines such as *Boy's Life* had a long history, but the new periodicals were unique in their focus on adolescence. Out of the comic book world came *Mad*, whose purposely sick humor and irreverent views had a wide influence, especially in exposing the weaknesses of adult society. Out of the realm of slick magazines came *Teen World*, *Modern Teen*, and *Teen Today*, especially designed to help adolescents relate both to their new selves and to their peers. Although they raised adult criticism that they reinforced the comformism and self-absorption so disturbingly prevalent among the young, the teen journals did provide answers to such important problems as shyness, social awkwardness, dress and appearance, and a hundred other matters of special torment. If nothing else, they took the teenager seriously, satisfying the need, wrote one reader, "to be appreciated for being a teen—not just tolerated by grown-ups until we, too, grow up."[4] This tendency to view the young as uniquely special was to be adopted by some more adult-oriented magazines in the 1960s.

The developing sense of teenage specialness received powerful support from music. Until the 1950s, musical tastes had been dominated by adults, but then the situation changed abruptly. When the rapid spread of television drastically reduced the number of radio listeners, radio broadcasters responded by concentrating on the new youth market and adjusting their music programming to its tastes. At the same time, the development of long-playing records and inexpensive record players greatly increased youth's access to recorded music; by the mid-1950s, teenagers were buying 43 percent of the records and 39 percent of the radios sold in America. With these media there came a musical message in the form of rock and roll, which first achieved notoriety in 1955 with Bill Haley's "Rock around the Clock." Before long, teenagers had their own music and also their own musical heroes, none more popular than Elvis Presley, who by 1959 had sold 35,000,000 records of his sometimes raunchy, sometimes sentimental songs. "Elvis the Pelvis," with his raw energy and defiant sexuality, demonstrated the appeal of rock and roll for youth. In contrast to the often soapy songs of the adult world, the new music seemed to harmonize with the inchoate energy and the concerns of adolescence. The fact that it frequently evoked strong expressions of loathing from adults only increased its appeal to the young.

The new music and the reactions to it seemed especially to mark a growing gap between the generations, evoking a widespread feeling that the young were evolving not only their own tastes but their own social and moral principles. The situation was actually more complex, however. Of greatest importance was the fact that the new teen influences had far less effect on the forties generation than on later baby boomers, those whose birth after 1952 exposed them more fully to the new influences, helping to create a separation within a generation that often included both older and younger siblings—though such differences were often overlooked by adults. Appropriating the idea of culture from the increasingly popular discipline of anthropology, some commentators began to speak of a "youth culture" or even a "contraculture." In 1959, James S. Coleman said that America and eventually other advanced societies were spawning "adolescent subcultures, with values and activities quite distinct from those

of adult society—subcultures whose members have most of their important associations within and few with adult society."[5] Coleman failed to
prove that such a distinct subculture actually existed, but he did strengthen
suspicions that adolescent peer groups, supported by teen fashions and
tastes, were indoctrinating their members with standards and values at
odds with those of their parents.

Much of the concern focused on the relationships between young males
and females. Although they involved the traditional stirrings of mysterious attractions, these relationships also reflected a basic change in sexual
attitudes, since youth was discovering its yearnings at a time when many
Americans had acquired the leisure and liberty to tease themselves with
thoughts about sex. In 1953, for instance, the first issue of *Playboy* marked
the advent of the playboy philosophy of human relations. The magazine
was one sign of an increasing interest in sexual matters, an interest sanctioned not only by the broad influence of Freudian psychology but also
by Alfred Kinsey's two surveys of the sexual behavior of American males
and females. Sex grew steadily as a matter of popular interest, leading a
sociologist to complain in 1954: "We talk too much about sex. We read
too much about it. Advertisements, magazine illustrations, television,
movies, popular songs glorify sexual love on all sides." Two years later,
another sociologist warned that America was undergoing a "sex revolution" characterized by "proliferating promiscuity" and by a growing "sex
addiction somewhat similar to drug addiction."[6]

Adults might accentuate the positive in this change when it related to
themselves, but they were less willing to extend the same privilege to their
children. Aside from their still strong acceptance of traditional sex values,
particularly as the basis for family life, they found several reasons to be
concerned about the sexuality of the young. By the mid-1950s, for instance, they took note of a steady increase in the incidence of venereal
disease (VD) among teenagers, after it seemed that penicillin had destroyed
that scourge; in 1959, parents were warned that VD had attained epidemic proportions in twenty-four cities and twenty-one states. And they
were alarmed by the increase in the number of illegitimate births among
teenage girls, a trend that prompted the Planned Parenthood Federation
in 1955 to call a conference to reconsider society's handling of abortion.
Parents who had believed these were lower-class problems found that they
were spreading among middle-class adolescents as well.

Such matters seemed to indicate that something like a revolution in
sexual attitudes was occurring among the young, and soon enough in the
1960s the idea would be publicized with a vengeance. For some parents,

however, sex took second place to another problem which, although still distant to the experience of most families, became increasingly threatening: the use of narcotics. Drug addiction was nothing new, but until the 1950s it had seemed to be fading from its strength earlier in the century. In World War I, one draftee of every 1,500 had been rejected as an addict; in World War II, the ratio fell to one of every 10,000. The early 1950s, however, brought an outburst of public anxiety over the alleged efforts of drug dealers who, with the dying-off of the older generation of addicts, were seeking to build a new clientele. The results included "children sniffing heroine in schoolrooms, dope peddlers invading playgrounds and coaxing children to try marijuana."[7]

At first, most observers treated drugs as a lower-class—especially black—issue, but uneasiness spread early in 1960 with the mass arrest of teenagers in two California cities for using narcotics. Soon thereafter, several teenagers were arrested for the same offense in New York's wealthy Westchester County, leading the father of one addict to warn that "drug addiction among teen-agers has become epidemic and is spreading into the 'fortunate' suburbs."[8] This was an exaggeration, but there seems little doubt that drug use in some areas was taking root as peer practice, an element in youth culture. Soon, the trend would spread into leading universities.

Throughout the 1950s, however, teenage addiction was overshadowed by even more extensive worries about teenage crime. The great majority of juvenile encounters with the law involved minor infractions, but a notable increase in violent behavior led one educator to warn that "the stage has been reached where frightful assaults, wanton acts of violence, and even murders are being perpetrated." In 1961, J. Edgar Hoover, head of the Federal Bureau of Investigation, declared that youth crime portended "a frightful internal crisis" toward which the nation was hurtling at perilous speed.[9] Such fears evoked much social analysis and soul searching, which affected not only the attitude of society toward the young but, eventually, the attitude of the young toward society. Some people traced delinquency to "permissiveness" and the general failure of parents to exercise proper authority. The principal causes, said Bishop Fulton Sheen, the popular television priest, were the "Doting, Drinking, and Divorce" of delinquent parents. Some blamed adult society in general. Especially common and also especially significant was the belief that most delinquency derived from the failure of society to provide youth with something better to do. Observers warned that modern society had unwittingly narrowed the road to adult competence and maturity for many of the young, thereby threatening to produce greater, perhaps even catastrophically greater, antisocial behavior in the decade ahead.

This line of thought led rather easily to the conclusion that the nation was confronted with a rising number of "alienated" youth engaged in what the journalist Harrison Salisbury called an "unconsciously anarchistic protest against the world as they perceive it." For many observers, this alienation could be cured if only society would act to provide avenues of opportunity for the deprived. A few radical thinkers, however, believed that the causes lay deeper in the essential character of society. In 1958, Edgar Z. Friedenberg in *The Vanishing Adolescent* condemned the adult world for engaging in a conspiracy, through its schools and other organizations, to suppress youth's natural desire for self-definition and an authentic life. Most of society's youthful victims remained passive in their alienation, but Friedenberg saw in those whom society labeled "delinquents" a heroic resistance, "a gallant if hopeless struggle with the timidity and corruption of the adult world."[10] His was an idea that would have wider use in the 1960s.

It was concern over youth alienation that brought to public attention one of the most important influences on the thinking of youth in the sixties: the publication of Paul Goodman's *Growing Up Absurd* in 1960 marked the beginning of a new era. Goodman, devoted adherent of the liberal-democratic-socialist-progressive outlook of the World War II era, insisted that juvenile delinquency was only one sign of a more fundamental youth problem created by existing society. For him, the "organized system" of large business corporations, government bureaucracies, and heavily administered schools which had grown to social dominance in the 1950s denied youth the opportunity to develop their characters and talents. Whereas the permissive and democratic family had allowed for the natural growth of the child, this system demanded conformity to its dictates at the expense of the opportunity "to grow up to be a man." By blocking the natural development of the young, society confronted them with the choice either of sacrificing their true selves to its demands or of rejecting it. Unless some fundamental change along democratic lines were made in the social order, America would confront increasing social disaffection on the part of its growing youth population.[11]

Obscured by complaints on both the right and the left was the fact that most of the new generation seemed ready to satisfy their parents' expectations. One study in 1959, for instance, found that many of the older teens, born in the early 1940s, took a serious interest in politics and hoped to make some improvement in society. Most were the more successful, college-bound products of the schools, young people determined not to be the adult caricature of themselves. Many were the products of democratic family life, the beneficiaries and inheritors of parental ideals. Although the progressive-democratic ideal had been dimmed by the McCarthy era, it survived in many families and schools. In their idealism, these young people often had the support and encouragement of adults who hoped they would carry out the reforms that the older generation had failed to achieve. If anything, criticism of their generation not only spurred them on to pursue their mission as democracy's children but provided them with accusations which by the mid-1960s they would turn against the accusers.

In 1959 the popular author Phyllis McGinley took stock of the middle-class youths whom she observed and concluded that "a notable generation was coming of age in our time." She found them energetic, eager to learn, moral, and "on fire to help a world which they certainly they had little share in making." They were contemptuous of materialism and moral compromise, ambitious to work for the good of others, especially for the victims of prejudice: "The thought of discriminating against a contemporary because of his color or religion is an offense. . . . Youth is living the great lesson it has truly learned—that all men are brothers."[12]

McGinley's glowing portrait was another partial truth about a complex generation, but it was affirmed in many ways: by a report in 1959 that, even with television, two of every three teenagers were currently reading a book outside of school, a record far better than that of the adult population; by the participation of some of the young in late 1950s demonstrations against racial segregation and for peace; by the efforts of a great many youth in numerous local voter-registration campaigns, civic improvement projects, and charity works throughout the country. When in 1960, *Parents Magazine* presented its annual awards for outstanding community service by youth groups, it issued 106 awards for such contributions as an antismoking campaign, a program to assist victims of cerebral palsy, and an effort to desegregate restaurants and stores.

The flow of constructive youth energies through such channels and through the various established organizations for the young helped satisfy some doubts about the next generation, but it also called attention to the failure of society to utilize fully the idealism and power of democracy's children. In 1959, for instance, a writer complained that adults had defeated an attempt by teenagers in a suburban community to organize efforts against both segregation and juvenile delinquency: "We are wasting enormous reservoirs of constructive energy and talent." Other adults agreed that the time had come to create new forms of youth involvement. The 1950s brought the formation of various youth councils and associations to involve teenagers in community affairs, as well as the management of their own special problems, on the principle, as one adult organizer put it, "that teen-agers have as much right to express their views as any other section of the population."[13] It was a principle that some young people were to carry into their college years in the 1960s, there to be both encouraged and condemned by the older generations.

A few adults presented ambitious plans for the restless young. In 1959, Harvey Swados, a veteran radical journalist and intellectual, proposed the formation of a volunteer force of at least 100,000 young people to work overseas for the improvement of underdeveloped nations, a project that he believed would fill a widespread need among the young for something worthy to do. The next year saw the submission to Congress of a more conservative proposal for an overseas "Youth Corps," which its sponsors said would provide its young recruits with a needed "sense of purpose—the excitement and stimulus of taking part in great events."[14] And so the idea of the Peace Corps was born.

The Peace Corps was one constructive channel for restless youth, but most of the new generation took their first steps toward maturity in the colleges and universities they had been prepared to enter. It was to the realm of higher education that democracy's children looked for freedom from the constraints of home and for avenues into a wider world. In fact, they found the academic world a new and complex reality, full of both promise and frustration, of both new freedoms and new restraints. One thing was evident: for good or ill, the full maturation of the young was delayed by these new years of education and dependence.

NOTES

1. National Council of State Committees for Children and Youth, *State Reports* (1960), 51.

2. Sloane Wilson, *The Man in the Gray Flannel Suit II* (New York, 1984), 37; Dale B. Harris, "Work and the Adolescent Transition to Maturity," in Robert E. Grinder, ed., *Studies in Adolescence* (New York, 1963), 148, 154, 160.

3. Gerald H. J. Pearson, *Adolescence and the Conflict of Generations* (New York, 1958), 148, 154, 160.

4. Charles H. Brown, "Self-Portrait: The Teen-Type Magazine," *Annals of the American Academy of Political and Social Sciences* 236 (1961): 13–21.

5. James S. Coleman, "The Adolescent Subculture and Academic Adjustment," *American Journal of Sociology* 65 (1959–60): 237–47; Milton Yinger,

"Contraculture and Subculture," *American Sociological Review* 25 (1960): 625–33.

6. Paul H. Landis, "Don't Expect Too Much of Sex in Marriage," *Reader's Digest* (December 1954): 25; Pitrim A. Sorokin, *The American Sex Revolution* (Boston, 1956), 12–14.

7. J. D. Ratcliff, "A Sane Look at Teen-Age Drug Addiction," *Parents Magazine* 26 (November 1951): 40-41; John Gerrity, "The Truth about the 'Drug Menace,' " *Harper's Magazine* 204 (February 1952): 27–31.

8. "My Son Was Caught Using Narcotics," *Saturday Evening Post* (December 10, 1960): 33.

9. J. Edgar Hoover, "These Fighters against Crime Need Your Help," *Reader's Digest* (April 1961): 145.

10. Harrison Salisbury, *The Shook-Up Generation* (New York, 1958), 209; Edgar Z. Friedenberg, *The Vanishing Adolescent*, 2d ed. (Boston, 1964), xiv, 6–11, 55–56, 66–67, 115–19.

11. Paul Goodman, *Growing Up Absurd* (New York, 1960), ix–xv, 11–15, 211, 241.

12. Phyllis McGinley, *The Province of the Heart* (New York, 1959), 41–49, 52.

13. Garrett Oppenheim, "What Youth Can Do When Grownups Help," *Parents Magazine* 34 (March 1959): 88–89, 125; Dorothy Siegel, "How Teens Can Help Themselves," *Parents Magazine* 35 (March 1960), 48–49, 102–6.

14. Harvey Swados, *A Radical's America* (Boston, 1962), 328, 332–35; Robert H. Bremner et al., eds., *Children and Youth in America* (Cambridge, MA, 1974), 3:258.

CHAPTER Four

SCALING THE IVIED WALLS

BY 1960 THE FORTIES GENERATION WAS BEGINNING TO ENTER American universities en masse, encountering a time of change that fortified both hopes and frustrations. In a complex, modern, urban-industrial order, those in their late teens or early twenties—who in earlier times would have entered the labor force and assumed adult responsibilities—now had to continue their education in the high schools and increasingly in the colleges and universities. This delayed entry into the real world complicated the problems of the restless young. "A sense of emptiness, restlessness, and prolonged dependence for youth," warned the educator, Kenneth Clark, "may be seen as a most powerful contemporary threat to the development of the creative aspect of their personality."[1]

Such concerns did not generally apply to lower- and working-class youth, who often were thrust into the adult world too soon but, except as juvenile delinquents, won far less public attention than the college-bound sons and daughters of the middle and upper classes. For middle-class youth especially, entry into maturity was made both more significant and more complicated by the fact that their first exposure to a social life beyond their families took place in an academic setting rather than in the workaday world. It was the college-bound young people who best exemplified the major trends of their times. This constantly expanding group began with the revolution in educational expectations that took place after World

War II; between 1940 and 1957 the proportion of Americans who graduated from college increased by more than 60 percent. Before the war the
benefits of college had been limited to a small minority, but the GI Bill
and other provisions for returning veterans allowed many more Americans to get a college education. In the later 1940s, as a result, the median
length of schooling for young adults increased by nearly two years, the
largest increase in the century.

The many men who had entered college under the GI Bill expected as
much or more education for *their* children. In middle-class families, college was becoming the norm, and plans for higher education became increasingly common among children of every class and color. These
expectations grew most notably among young women. Beginning in the
late 1950s the enrollment of women in college increased at a faster rate
than that of men, reversing the trend of previous decades: the proportion
of women to men in college declined from 40 to 60 in 1939 to 35 to 65 in
1958. These figures reflected the great increase in the number of male
students, however, not a decrease in the absolute number of females. By
the late 1960s the 1940 proportion had been reestablished, with more
than 1,600,000 women in full-time attendance.

In 1963, 75 percent of high school boys and 69 percent of girls said
that they expected to attend college. The percentage of those who actually enrolled in higher education was considerably lower but still significant: Whereas in the late 1930s, only one in seven high school graduates
went on to college, more than one in three of a much larger number did so
in the early 1960s. The rising percentage of college-bound youth coupled
with the rapidly growing number of youth threatened to engulf the system of higher education: "Unless we already have begun to build our
arks," wrote one professor in 1957, "we are sure to go under when the
big wave hits."[2] The response was a rapidly expanding number of educational arks, enough to absorb the 117 percent increase in enrollments that
took place in the decade after 1955.

The rapid growth of the college-bound population generated a highly
competitive situation, which had a mixed effect on both students and
higher education. By the late 1950s, ambitious parents and their children
had been alerted to the intense competition for admission to the most
selective colleges and universities. In response, the better public schools,
especially in suburbia, upgraded their college preparatory programs.
Backed by warnings that preparation for college should begin not later
than the eighth or ninth grade, parents applied pressure both on their
children and on the schools to excel, receiving support from the post-

Sputnik emphasis on educational excellence. It was a time of much talk about the need to create a "meritocracy" of the best and brightest people, and some of the baby boomers seemed to measure up to meritocratic hopes.

One college president said that the new students had a much greater appreciation of higher learning than the old, and a spokesman for the National Education Association spoke fervently of a "fired-up generation ... thirsty for knowledge and experience."[3] Competitive pressures brought results. The average scores on the Scholastic Aptitude Test among students accepted by the selective colleges skyrocketed; at Harvard, it rose by 90 points, or 15 percent, between 1956 and 1959. At Kent State University in Ohio the proportion of freshmen with B or better high school averages grew from 42 percent in 1959 to 79 percent in 1962, thanks to the elimination of open admissions there. Taking advantage of the intensifying competition, many colleges and universities adopted admissions policies designed to upgrade the overall quality of their new students; less prestigious institutions strove for the same end by admitting all applicants and then flunking out a large percentage of them.

Unwittingly, the universities created a situation that would make this important step toward maturity a frustrating if not alienating experience for many students. Having worked so hard to be admitted into ivied halls, young Americans often found much less than they had expected. Dissatisfaction was strongest and most significant among those students admitted to the major universities, producing waves of discontent that set the pace and direction for student movements in the sixties. The students admitted to these universities tended to be not only the brightest but the most serious-minded students, a generation which had little use for the fraternities, sororities, football, and the rah-rah spirit that had exercised youthful energies in the past. Encouraged by the current stress on excellence, they wanted to study with the best minds of America. Instead, they were thrust into a heavily institutionalized setting that seemed both to offer and deny the enlightenment they sought.

The decade after 1960 was the heyday of the "multiversity," the university with multiple roles, only one of which was to teach students. Clark Kerr, president of the University of California at Berkeley, declared in 1963 that the multiversity was at the center of the "knowledge industry," generating the new knowledge required for modern progress and providing the intellectual know-how needed to resolve modern problems. It had also become a major player in the Cold War, serving as "an instrument of national purpose, a component part of the 'military industrial complex.' "

The resulting research contracts and grants greatly benefited the major universities and many of their professors, but these functions also compounded the problem of teaching a growing mass of bright, ambitious students. As Kerr recognized, the incorporation of professors into the research-oriented knowledge industry meant their removal from the teaching process. The resulting large classes, often indifferent teaching, and neglect of student needs generated resentment among new students: "There is an incipient revolt of undergraduates against the faculty."[4]

Kerr soon discovered at Berkeley that the student revolt was directed less against the faculty than against administrators like himself, but he had rightly diagnosed the situation. Although most students found no reason to revolt, particularly those in business and engineering, many in the social sciences and humanities were disposed to resentment and protest. These were students who had looked forward to what they assumed would be an exciting new phase of education in which they would find understanding of themselves and of society. Instead, they were required to take classes that seemed only to repeat what they had learned in high school and from private reading or were perversely remote from what they wanted to know. Eager to learn about the real life from which they were removed by their extended youth, they encountered a world of specialized scholarship where, as student leader Tom Hayden put it in 1962, social reality was "objectified" into sterility. Such encounters only deepened the suspicion, which many had already acquired from progressive schooling, of impersonal and abstract truths. Generalized truths of this sort, no matter how valid, were no substitutes for practical understandings of society and of themselves.

If they rejected the subject matter presented by the "Establishment," they also grew resentful of the way it was presented. In the university classroom they were often only numbers in a crowd of anonymous students exposed to a ruthless grading system that pitted the best and brightest against one another in a competition where only the few could shine. It was a vastly different world from the democratic families in which many had been raised and where they had often been encouraged to speak out on subjects of importance—to the point, complained the psychologist Abraham Maslow, that his students at Brandeis University had been brought up to expect to talk while their elders listened: "They want my ear, not what I can say" was a common lament among college professors which served to deepen the stress between the generations.[5]

Although most students acquiesced to what seemed to be the inevitable, a significant minority developed a loathing for what they came to see as a bureaucratic system that denied their existence as individuals. As one of them described it, the university was a machine that subjected its victims to a "spiritual brutality inflicted by a faculty of well-meaning and nice men who give you forty courses, one hundred and twenty units, fifteen hundred to two thousand lectures, and over three hundred over-sized discussions."[6] Soon, such feelings would ripen into a downright hatred of the System, turning them against civil government and the liberal establishment that often guided it.

What to do? Some of the dissenters simply dropped out of school, more than a few directing their opposition to the larger society, which they believed the university served; others joined the expanding ranks of "beatniks" and "hippies." Many of those who stayed demanded basic changes in the educational process: more flexible requirements, smaller classes, fewer lectures, the elimination of compulsory attendance, the modification if not the termination of the grading system, and their own right to grade their professors. Above all, they demanded some student input into higher education so that they could exercise over their immediate worlds the influence promised by the democratic ideal.

When the institutions were slow to act, some students drifted into educational fantasies of student-centered universities where everyone would be actively involved in learning what was relevant and where the needs of the learner would count for more than pedagogical wisdom. In this they had the support of Paul Goodman, whose combination of educational progressivism and anarchistic opposition to bigness appealed to their growing antipathy toward institutions. In 1962, Goodman urged dissenting students and sympathetic faculty to create their own schools along the lines of medieval universities: "This spontaneous quest by the anarchic early community of scholars to understand their culture and take responsibility for changing it should be ours as well." By the mid-1960s, dissidents began to form "free universities" such as Dartmouth Experimental College in New Hampshire, which proclaimed it had "no grades, no exams, no credits. Just bring enthusiasm and a desire to learn."[7] Such schools generally invited students to design their own courses, directed to their interests and needs.

Most dissenting students, however, remained with the degree-granting institutions, where they attempted with considerable success to change not only the formal system of education but also the "second curriculum" of the university, the highly influential collegiate social world outside the classroom. Especially in the early years, their efforts often won some approval from the universities. In the 1950s student life in

many institutions had become even less intellectual, leading one professor
to complain that "our campuses are becoming marriage mills and fun
factories, more devoted to beauty queens than to higher education." These
were times when student rebelliousness took the form of "fun" riots and
panty raids, annoyances that one observer attributed to biological causes
similar "to the rutting of the buck deer and the vernal craziness of the
ruffed grouse."[8]

Change came with the appearance on campus of democracy's children, many of whom were serious-minded students whose educational
discontents often brought them into conflict with traditional student society. In 1960, for instance, a survey of 250 entering "war babies" at
Swarthmore College found them intellectually active and much interested
in learning about, as one put it, "things that will enable us to straighten
out the world." Such students did much to challenge the flabby academic
culture of American universities. In 1962 the National Student Association (NSA), speaking for the serious-minded, complained that American
colleges "lack devotion to the intellect" and blamed them for allowing
the distracting presence of social and athletic activities that had nothing
to do with education.[9] Such critics were not new, but the sheer size of the
new student population significantly increased their critical mass, creating a strong challenge to prevailing collegiate social practice.

Much of their opposition focused on a role that American colleges
had long played, one summed up by the phrase *in loco parentis*. Young
people with little Latin and some humor saw "crazy parents" in that term,
but it signified the sober claim of colleges to some of the rights and responsibilities of a parent vis-à-vis their students. Originating and maintained in large part to assure anxious parents that their children, especially
daughters, would be safe from physical and moral damage, the role was
generally benign. Out of it developed an ever growing number of campus
counselors, physicians, and psychologists who, along with marching bands
and football teams, made the American college something more and less
than an institution of higher learning. Few students objected to such services, but many chafed at the various efforts to regulate their lives that
came with this paternalism.

Former generations of students had taken great delight in ignoring
college regulations whenever possible, especially those relating to drinking and dating. Among the new students, however, dissenters chose the
more radical tack of calling for the elimination of such restrictions on the
grounds that they were undemocratic and an affront to individual dignity. In this, they had the support of the NSA, which in 1961 condemned

the *in loco parentis* doctrine on the grounds that it denied students the freedom they needed to mature, socially as well as intellectually. They condemned the long-established presumption that as students they did not enjoy basic legal rights when they were subjected to campus discipline or dismissal. They objected to university regulations requiring that they live in dormitories and regulating their behavior in the dormitory setting. They called for an end to curfews and restrictions on visits between the sexes, and some began to demand coeducational dormitories and other living facilities that they could choose for themselves.

The attack on *in loco parentis* encountered strong resistance from college administrators, concerned with allaying the fears of parents and maintaining campus order. Much of the concern of parents arose out of what was coming to be called the sexual revolution. Undoubtedly, many adults shared the alarm of Jennie Loitman Barron, a Massachusetts judge, who complained in 1964 that colleges were failing in their duty to teach students how to control their sex drives: "At all too many colleges today, sexual promiscuity among students is a dangerous and growing evil."[10] In the eyes of anxious adults, the campuses seemed much too supportive of sexual innovation and rebellion against traditional values.

In the eyes of students attuned to democratic values, though, resistance to their demands was another example of the System's refusal to recognize their freedom and dignity. This attitude found some encouragement within the universities. While the administrative system might seem repressive, the academic setting introduced large numbers of young men and women to new ideas regarding human freedom. For example, students encountered the sexual radicalism of Norman O. Brown and Herbert Marcuse, whose books—*Life against Death* and *Eros and Civilization*—had been published in the 1950s. Few may have really understood the sexual mysticism in Brown or the mixture of Marx and Freud in Marcuse, but they could appreciate the contention of both men that the repression of sexual urges was a major cause of human misery. Anthropology, with its investigation of exotic cultures, perhaps had an even wider influence. "No student who has studied the sexual practices in this and other cultures," wrote Paul Woodring in 1968, "is likely to believe that monogamous marriage is the only outlet for sex that can be defended."[11]

These ideas were part of a more general "new" morality that seemed to be gaining wide influence among students at the expense of the old emphasis on obedience to established moral rules. Although the 1950s had seen a revival of interest in traditional religion on many campuses, this trend was soon countered by newer interests in existentialist philosophy and God-is-dead theology. Especially at the major universities, students took it as an obligation as well as a right to challenge conventional moral thinking. The most common result was a moral individualism which held that each person should decide for himself what was appropriate to a particular circumstance rather than adhering to established moral rules. This attitude was formalized as situational ethics and denounced as an easy-going relativism. Generally, it was linked to a single principle that anything was morally acceptable if it did not hurt another person. It was a simple code suited to the protected existence of most students, but its extreme was an irresponsible egotism that rarely went beyond an emphasis on "my rights."

In most cases, however, the new morality was less a revolution than a stage in a liberalization of attitudes that had been under way in society for several generations, one that favored a more open acceptance of sexuality as natural and good but did not generally approve of promiscuity. A 1964 study of college women, for instance, concluded that three-quarters of the unmarried ones were virgins and that most of the rest had had intercourse only with their future husbands. Overall, parents seemed to have been more successful in morally educating their children than they feared. Moreover, the new morality had its strongest influence among dissenting students in the major universities, those who had often been raised with a concern for democratic social and political values that served as a check on moral egotism.

This concern bubbled to the surface at the very beginning of the 1960s. By this time, Americans were awakening from the social stupor of the McCarthy era. During those years, there had been considerable hand-wringing over the so-called silent generation, whose political passivity led Edward R. Murrow to fear that the colleges were producing a generation that would shun controversy and "not ask the tough or embarrassing question."[12] The end of the 1950s, however, brought stirrings of activity, including a growing assertiveness of student newspapers on some of the major campuses. These papers were important training grounds for young leaders such as Tom Hayden, editor of the *Michigan Daily*, and a not insignificant influence on public opinion; in the 1960s there were some 1,800 college dailies with a combined circulation of close to 6 million. The times also brought efforts to transform the tasks of student government associations from "sandbox" exercises into active representation of student interests. On some few campuses, students organized political parties to fight for their rights and for curricular reforms. These also involved a growing interest in outside politics: in 1961 alone, political clubs of various persuasions were formed on more than 300 campuses. These developments, undoubtedly a long overdue response to bland times, marked the appearance of democracy's children and their values on campus.

At the opening of the 1960s, there was some uncertainty over the direction the student awakening would take. In early 1961, *Time* magazine predicted "a sharp swing to the right" among students, who it believed would react, as the young were expected to do, against the political beliefs of their—generally liberal—parents. In the same year, the conservative thinker M. Stanton Evans saw signs of a "campus revolt" against New Deal liberalism: "Young people are interested in things which are bright, lively, and diverting. And the sonorous repetitions of Liberalism are none of these. It is dead on his feet."[13] Evans and others took special note of student interest in Barry Goldwater's book *The Conscience of a Conservative* (1960), and of the aggressive activity of the newly formed Young Americans for Freedom (YAF), which planned to seize control of the NSA.

The long term was to give some credence to conservative hopes, but even before Evans published his *Revolt on Campus* (1961), it was evident that the strongest winds were blowing the other way. Studies made at the time suggested that college students tended to accept the influence of a generally liberalism-oriented faculty; one study indicated that of every three students who changed their politics in college, two adopted more liberal views. In the summer of 1960 the NSA president, Donald A. Hoffman, boasted that his generation was no longer silent on social issues: "Many college students are fed up with the way things are going." In August 1961 the annual NSA convention confirmed Hoffman's judgment by rejecting a YAF effort, as liberal journalist Jack Newfield put it, "to lead the nation's youth into the nineteenth century."[14] Observers noted that although the student delegates were not flaming radicals, the majority identified with liberal causes.

The new protesters gave special attention to attacking the Cold War mentality that had dampened American thought and imagination throughout most of the 1950s. They condemned the requirement that students seeking federal educational assistance disclaim any association with supposedly subversive organizations, and they denounced the House Un-American Affairs Committee (HUAC), which had carried its hunt for subversives into the universities. Student newspapers and the NSA condemned HUAC as a threat to freedom of thought and discussion, and students jeered at the committee's film *Operation Abolition*, which did more to convert them to anti-anticommunism than to its version of patriotism. Some of them demonstrated against nuclear testing and for world peace, and in February 1961 more than 5,000 students from 100 colleges converged on Washington, DC, to express their opposition to Cold War militancy. Steven V. Roberts, editor of the *Harvard Crimson*, said that most of the protesters belonged to the category "realistic liberal," young people moved by the feeling that something had to be done to shake the decision-makers into a response to popular concerns: "There is a desperate feeling among politically concerned students that the traditional democratic process must be rescued."[15]

The protesters were a small minority among students. A survey of opinion at sixteen colleges in the fall of 1961 found that only 17 percent of students held that war was contrary to their moral beliefs, and most continued to regard communism as a greater danger than war. Nevertheless, the protest movement had special strength in many of the leading universities where the nation's future leaders, its brightest youth, had gathered. As had happened in the past, an active, idealistic minority promised to leave its stamp on both the present and the future, marking a new age.

The new student activism quickly raised the thought—already a cliché among those concerned with adolescent behavior—that it was a rebellion of the young against their parents, but this was not generally the case. There was no doubt plenty of rebelliousness against parents, but it was likely to be expressed in nonpolitical ways—in delinquency and in drink and drugs rather than in demonstrations for peace and human rights. Two psychiatrists rightly concluded that the natural striving of the young for an identity apart from parents involved "both identification with and rebellion against parents and past." Even though some youthful activists took pride in going beyond what they thought was the timidity and inertia of their parents, most came from democratic households whose values they espoused. In the early 1960s, Kenneth Keniston, a leading authority on youth, described what he thought was the typical activist student: "His activism is more often premised upon the liberal values of his parents and the credal values of American society than opposed to them. Indeed if there is any psychological thread that runs through student activism today, it is this identification with parental values. When parents and their activist offspring disagree, it is usually not over principle but practice."[16]

Certainly, the student awakening of the early 1960s seems to have been primarily a renewal of earlier commitments to liberal democracy. As such, it received strong adult support, including that of the majority of some forty American educators who, when polled on their views of the young, expressed satisfaction that youth was ceasing to be the silent generation and becoming a force for progress, opening new channels for social protest and change. Most of this promise adhered to the majority of democracy's children who were white and middle class. In 1960, however, an especially momentous new channel was opened from a new direction, the work of one cohort of the forties generation that had grown up, with little general notice, in a world set apart from the world of the majority.

NOTES

1. Kenneth Clark, "Present Threats to Children and Youth," in Bremner et al., *Children and Youth*, 3:164.

2. Richard H. Hill, "More on the Tidal Wave," *School and Society* 85 (1957): 75.

3. *New York Times* (March 18, 1962): 77; Laurence Siegel et al., "Burgeoning University Enrollments and Academic Quality," *School and Society* 91 (1963): 338.

4. Clark Kerr, *The Uses of the University—With a Postscript—1972* (Cambridge, MA, 1972), 18, 52–53, 88, 103, 124.

5. A. H. Maslow, *Journals*, ed. Richard L. Lowrey (Monterey, CA, 1974), 1:515.

6. Asa S. Knowles, "Changes in the Traditional Concept of Higher Education," *School and Society* 98 (1971): 406–8; Edward E. Sampson, "Student Activism and the Decade of Protest," *Journal of Social Issues* 23, no. 3 (1967): 21–24.

7. Paul Goodman, "For a Reactionary Experiment in Education," *Harper's Magazine* 223 (1966): 61–72; Robert H. Farber, "The Free University," *School and Society* 97 (1962): 356–58.

8. Jerome Ellison, "Are We Making a Playground out of College?" *Saturday Evening Post* (April 28, 1956): 26–27.

9. Kenneth Keniston, "The Faces in the Lecture Room," in Robert S. Morrison, ed., *The Contemporary University* (Boston, 1956), 329–30; Russell Kirk, *Decadence and Renewal in the Higher Learning* (South Bend, IN, 1978), 79.

10. Jennie L. Barron, "Too Much Sex on Campus," *Reader's Digest* (May 1964): 59–62.

11. Paul Woodring, *The Higher Learning in America* (New York, 1968), 110.

12. Quoted in "Higher Learning and the Future," *School and Society* 89 (1961): 435–36.

13. M. Stanton Evans, *Revolt on Campus* (Chicago, 1961), 46.

14. Jack Newfield, "The Real Revolt on Campus," *Commonweal* 75 (1961): 309–11.

15. Peter Schrang, "Stirrings on Campus," *New Republic* (April 17, 1961): 9–10; Steven Roberts, "Something Had to Be Done," *The Nation* 194 (1962): 187–90.

16. Keniston, "Faces in the Lecture Room," 337–38.

CHAPTER **Five**

IN DIVERSITY, SEPARATION

IN DEMOCRATIC AMERICA THE IDEAL WAS EQUALITY AND UNITY, YET the social reality was often inequality and separation. That reality was frequently obscured by the almost obsessive interest during the 1950s in the burgeoning suburban middle class with its modest affluence, its family orientation, and its child-centered practices. Apart from the suburbs, however, there were other worlds where children were born, raised, and educated; most of the young grew up on farms or in villages or in the diverse milieus of cities great and small. Along with this diversity there was much inequality of status, power, and opportunity. In 1950 the United States Children's Bureau estimated that some 10 percent of the nation's children lived in affluent families whose annual cash incomes ranged upward from $6,000, occasionally to the level of superwealth hidden discreetly in exclusive suburbs and exclusive institutions. At the other extreme, more than 25 percent of American youth lived in families with incomes of $2,000 *or less.*

These figures expressed a class society of rich people and poor people, of upper, upper-middle, middle-middle, lower-middle, and working classes and, below, the gray gradients of the poor down to a level waiting to be named the "underclass." At least occasionally, Americans took note of class differences in child-raising. Below the mysterious family world of the rich with its nannies, governesses, and private schools, the biggest difference observed was between the middle and working classes. At least two separate studies in the 1950s revealed that whereas middle-class parents tended to be permissive and democratic in line with current child-rearing doctrine, the working class emphasized obedience to parental authority, generally with the assistance of physical punishment as opposed to the persuasive techniques favored by the middle class.

These distinctive ways of preparing children for life highlighted expected differences among the classes: different opportunities, different social environments, different schooling, different jobs, and different social destinies. Whatever the effects of class on equality of opportunity, however, they were decisively overshadowed by the far deeper inequality of racial caste which the nation had inherited from a deeply racist past. Although midcentury America might profess itself to be a society of equals, few could deny that the substantial minority of Americans who happened to be black were socially separate and unequal, part but also *not* part of a country that continued to define itself as a white nation. "We are all engaged," said one observer, "all caught up in a web of belief and habit that sets Negroes and most whites apart from each other, makes communication between them awkward, complicates negotiation and compromise, and renders difficult the making of genuine friendships across the boundary."[1]

This social separation affected the ways in which blacks participated in the dominant movements of the times. Like whites during the postwar decades, blacks often migrated to new places, but their primary road ran from the rural South to the inner cities rather than from cities to suburbs: what at the beginning of the century had been the most rural of American populations was becoming the most citified. Like whites, blacks participated in the baby boom, their increase in births roughly paralleling that of whites, though their birthrate had been and remained higher than that of whites: at the 1950 rate, the black population was expected to grow twice as fast as the white population. Like whites, they saw a substantial reduction in infant mortality during the 1940s, but their infant mortality rate remained more than 70 percent higher than that of whites. Like whites, they achieved considerable gains in education, adding more than two years to their average length of schooling between 1940 and 1960, yet in the latter year the typical nonwhite male adult still remained nearly three years behind the typical white. In others ways, too, they reaped the benefits of progress only to remain as far behind as before.

Separateness was also reflected in class and family relationships. The class structure of black America mirrored in a distorted way the white class system: at the top a tiny number of wealthy blacks emulated the life-styles of white wealth. Below them, a larger number of middle-class black professionals, small business people, clerical workers, and skilled trades-men often had an even fiercer devotion to work, morality, and family life than did the white middle class. And at the bottom was a majority of poor and culturally depressed people whose social and economic problems were often even more intense than those of the white poor. It was this dispro-portionately large class of rural and urban poor that produced the often noted social differences between the black and white populations, espe-cially the higher black birthrate, the greater mortality of black babies and mothers, and the disproportionate number of illegitimate births. The class situation was also the chief reason that a substantial number of nonwhite children grew up in one-parent households. In 1950, somewhat less than 10 percent of all American children were in broken families, compared with 40 percent for blacks—the great majority in families headed by women. And the situation worsened over the next decades, producing the famed warning of the sociologist Daniel Moynihan in the 1960s that the poor black family was in the process of a total breakdown.

The combination of class and family circumstances made life difficult enough for most black youth, but, worse, *all* blacks were imprisoned in a pervasive system of racism and racial discrimination. Aside from the usual problems of parenting, black parents had the painful task of preparing their children to cope with a society that seemed bent on humiliating and frustrating them. While white parents could concentrate on promoting the development of a positive self-image in their children, a black parent awaited with bitterness and anxiety the day when her child would first collide with the barrier of race, perhaps hearing a white boy ask his mother, "Why does that boy have a dirty face?"

Black parents responded in various ways. There were those who, in effect, taught their children to accept the white racist belief that blacks were inferior, leading some into sullen resignation and others to dream of "passing" into the dominant caste. At the other extreme, some parents inculcated a fierce pride in their race. Others, especially in the middle class, focused on preparing their children for a life of achievement despite the barriers of race. Whatever else they did, they taught their children to be wary of the white population. "White people are a real danger to us until we learn how to live with them," said one southern mother. "So if you want your kids to live long, they have to grow up scared of whites." Especially among the poor, such training tended to be harsh and rigid, a sharp slap for the child whose failure to toe the line threatened to antagonize whites. The black sociologist E. Franklin Frazier said that black parents "caution their children to avoid conflicts, to ignore insults, and to adopt techniques for 'getting by.' These techniques include 'acting like a monkey,' 'jibing,' flattery, and plain lying."[2] Other techniques were more subtle but to the same effect: ways to be self-effacing, to be unnoticed by whites as much as possible.

There was no way to escape from a racist society and its influences. In public life, white heroes and leaders predominated; in advertisements and commercials, white families and their ways prevailed. Teachers were white and policemen were white. Even where racism was not overt, the message was that white people were the real people, the ones deserving of God's grace and society's blessings, whereas, in the words of a contemporary rhyme, "the people who are brown—they have to go down."[3] Little wonder that black children often wished to belong to the other race and preferred light skin to dark skin. In test after test, when given a choice, many black children chose to play with white dolls rather than with black and to identify white as good and black as not.

What chance, then, did they have for happiness and success in this society? Not all was negative; many black parents did help their children develop a positive view of themselves, often by pointing out the proud history of their people. Robert Cole, a sensitive white expert on black childhood, said that blacks not only showed a toughness in resisting the psychological oppressions of racism but often found in their race a basis for definite self-identity, whereas whites often had to struggle to find out who they were. But those pluses, though real, did not balance out the fact that the same society that prided itself on equal opportunity for all created debilitating conditions of inequality for black children.

Inequality remained a dominant fact of life even after black people fled from the segregated South to northern cities; there, a less visible pattern of discrimination nevertheless penned up the majority in urban ghettos, in a dismal subculture of low incomes, little education, broken families, and bad housing, of rats and dirt and crowding and crime. The existence of such areas largely explain why in the 1950s, for instance, black people in New York City committed, on a per capita basis, three times as many crimes and had eight times as many illegitimate births as the white population. The stark contrast between black ghetto and white suburb had become a stereotype in social thought by the late 1950s. By any measure, the ghetto was a bad environment for children to grow up in, one that tested even the strongest resolve to survive with dignity and hope.

In theory, there were at least two major avenues out of the slums and into a better life, but both were constricted by effects of poverty and racism. One was education. Northern urban schools had at least avoided the outright segregation by law that still prevailed in the South, but poor black children in both sections received an inferior education. Coming from culturally, economically, and socially deprived families, city children were crowded into rundown, poorly funded ghetto schools. Hampered by troubled home lives, many children quickly fell behind. One study revealed that black sixth graders had, on the average, reading scores nearly two grades below those of whites. Another study discovered that by age sixteen, nonwhite males had completed almost two fewer school grades than whites; still another evoked the claim that in the black schools of New York City the IQ of students had "actually deteriorated from year to year."[4]

Although many black students did manage to get a good education, the fact remained that a disturbingly high proportion of black teenagers learned little of what society was prepared to teach, and at a time when education was becoming increasingly necessary for the second way out of poverty: a decent job. Frustrated with a schooling that meant little but trouble, many teenagers dropped out at the first opportunity, only to find that they could not find legitimate paid employment. In one large ghetto in 1960, some 63 percent of male dropouts from school were unemployed. Unfortunately, in such areas even a high school degree often meant little; some 48 percent of graduates were unemployed, victims of their own poor training as well as racial discrimination in hiring. Further, not only was black youth unemployment higher than that of whites to begin with but it rose faster in the 1950s; by the early 1960s it was nearly twice that of white teenagers, and the problem promised to get worse as baby boomers crowded the job market in increasing numbers.

The narrowness of both the educational and vocational exit channels left a great many young ghetto dwellers with no constructive way out of their situation. The result was trouble, especially for teenage males. Often reared in broken families where discipline was authoritarian but increasingly ineffectual, many developed a contempt for all authority. Spending much of their lives in the streets, they became strongly bonded to peer groups whose primary models were likely to be the pimps and petty thieves of the neighborhood. Many drifted into early delinquency; the rate of juvenile delinquency among black males was about twice that of white males (though the estimated rate for black girls was actually lower than for white girls). They often found their real families in the various street gangs, which grew in size and numbers as the ghettos grew. Like white gangs, most of these gangs spent more time struggling to avoid boredom than anything else, but the potential for violence and crime was there. In the late 1950s an observer of one ghetto gang, the Cobras, described its character: "They live a life which touches the ordinary adult world only along the edges. Theirs is a subculture, a subculture with its own mores, codes, ceremonies, language and interests. The Cobras do not know what goes on in the other world nor do they care. . . . Beset by force and violence, they escape into paranoid visions of grandeur, daydreams of demonic power, ecstasies of sadism, endless fantasies with a gun."[5]

Equally alienated were the "cool" or "hip" youth who attempted to escape from society to a world of immediate gratification, to thrills and "kicks," freewheeling sexual experience, music, alcohol, and drugs. Contemptuous of the world of "squares," they evolved their own dress styles and their own vocabulary oriented toward sex and drugs. To support their habits, they specialized in petty thievery and various hustles or cons to cheat the unwary. This was the world that first experienced the upswing of drug usage after World War II. The author Claude Brown, who along with his hip friends smoked marijuana as a boy, said that by the early 1950s "heroin had just about taken over Harlem. It seemed like a plague."[6] In its drug use, its hot and cool jazz, its apparently uninhibited sexuality, and its contempt for straight society, the hip style appealed also to many romantically inclined whites, who, disgusted with the middle class and its life-style, added to the ferment that was to produce the counterculture of the 1960s.

The majority of black youth in America did not belong to either the gang or the cool culture, but the demographics of the 1950s tended to favor the rapid growth of both forms of adolescent alienation. Even though in 1950 nearly three-quarters of black teenagers still lived in the South, the combination of the black migration to the cities and the rapid rise in the black birthrate during the baby boom brought an extraordinary increase in the number of ghetto youth over the next decades. In the 1940s, while the number of nonwhite children under five grew by only 12 percent in the South, this future teenage population increased by well over 100 percent in northern cities, most of it in the urban ghettos. The results were increasing pressures on both the schools and the youth job market and growing tensions within the ghettos, which were to explode with society-shaking violence in the 1960s.

This potential, however, was obscured in the 1950s by a far more positive trend, the first major signs of the breakdown of the segregation and institutionalized discrimination that formed the basis of the caste system. The World War II period had brought a significant (though by no means total) change of heart in white America. Having defeated the racism of Adolph Hitler and seen its grim results, many whites were less willing to tolerate their own intolerance, especially since their black countrymen had helped win the war. Moreover, victory had ushered the United States into an era when the nonwhite people of the world were destined to play increasingly important roles. With the outbreak of the Cold War, white America began to recognize that its racist past was a serious handicap in the competition with the Soviet Union for the support of nonaligned peoples.

These influences brought no magical conversion, but they did initiate a strong new trend against discrimination, which would gain momentum in the postwar decades. Advocates of equal rights recognized the special importance of preparing the next generation for a tolerant society, for completing what in 1946 the sociologist Louis Wirth called the "unfinished business of American democracy." "There is a little hope for our grownups," wrote one advocate, "but in our children lies the big hope. While they are young and suggestible, before their thinking jells and their feelings curdle, we can give them some tools for building 'America for everybody.' "[7] Especially in democratic households and progressive schools, adults responded to the call for equality by educating their children to the principles of justice and fair play which their own upbringing in a racist society had kept them from fully practicing. This tendency to preach more than practice helped justify later complaints by the young about the hypocrisy of adults, but it also marked a significant change in public attitudes. In 1942, when asked whether blacks were as intelligent as whites, only 42 percent of adult whites in a national poll answered in the affirmative; by 1956 the figure had risen to 78 percent. Over the same period the percentage of whites opposed to segregation on streetcars and buses rose from 44 to 60 percent.

The 1950s also saw a most significant triumph for equality in the realm of education. It was natural that the child-centered society of the times should be sensitive about racism in the classroom, which threatened both to impair black children psychologically and to miseducate whites. Segregation in schooling seemed especially bad, since black schoolchildren rarely received their fair share of public funds and support, despite the legal fiction of "separate but equal" schools. A growing number of white Americans agreed that such an unjust system had to go if public education was, as one put it in 1952, to "provide equal opportunities for democracy's children" and to prepare "youth for democratic living."[8] When asked whether they favored integrated or segregated schools, 66 percent of white Americans in 1942 said they favored separate schools, but by 1956 the proportion had declined to slightly less than half; significantly, a 1954 poll of high school students of all races indicated that less than one-quarter of the young favored segregation.

This trend received powerful support in the 1954 Supreme Court ruling against segregated schools as inherently unequal. In stating the opinion of the Court, Chief Justice Earl Warren reiterated the conclusion of a lower court that segregation, with its presumption of racial inferiority, was detrimental to black children: "A sense of inferiority affects the motivation of a child to learn. Segregation with the sanction of law, therefore, has a tendency to retard the educational and mental development of Negro children." The 1954 decision opened a new phase in the advance of civil rights marked by decisions against segregation in public transportation and discrimination in voting. In the mid-1950s, even under a conservative national administration, progress was such as to persuade the National Association for the Advancement of Colored People (NAACP) to make 1963, the centennial of the Emancipation Proclamation, its deadline for the "elimination of second-class citizenship in the United States."[9] New times were coming.

Progress, however, often lagged behind expectations, largely because of the stubborn resistance of the segregationist South. Beyond traditional legal remedies, progress seemed to demand new and more direct tactics, and in 1956 that need was met by the successful nonviolent boycott against segregation on city buses in Montgomery, Alabama. Initiated and maintained by blacks and headed by the inspired new black leader Martin Luther King Jr., the boycott opened the way for the involvement of ordinary black people in their own emancipation from the racist past. The new way especially attracted the attention of black youth, in part because it answered their need for something worthy to do, and they soon established a pattern of behavior that many of their white peers were to follow with great vigor in the 1960s. The young first entered on the public stage primarily as unwilling martyrs to angry white resistance to school integration. Their most publicized entry was at Little Rock, Arkansas, where in 1957 nine carefully chosen black girls and boys defied the fury of white mobs to enter the newly integrated Central High School. It took the presence of the 101st Airborne Division, sent to the city by President Dwight Eisenhower, to protect their right to a good high school education.

In early 1960 the emerging new generation took the initiative when students at black colleges in the South began a dramatic sit-in campaign against segregation. Most of the students came from the black middle class, whose rapid growth in the postwar era had helped create a hopeful climate for positive change. Freed from the direct oversight of their more cautious parents, young men and women at America's numerous black residential colleges could organize for independent action. Although there had been some student action in the 1950s—in 1956, students at Florida A&M College in Tallahassee had boycotted segregated buses—it was 1960 that brought the new movement into existence with the launching of the first sit-in by students at North Carolina A&T College in Greensboro.

The college, itself a segregated institution, provided a meeting ground for a small group of black students who discovered a common resentment of the racist system. Amid the general apathy of the A&T student body, they began to discuss what to do. When one of them suggested that they try to have lunch at a segregated Greensboro restaurant, they hesitated, fearing arrest and probably a physical beating, but each felt compelled to act in answer to the question that challenged them all: "Are you or aren't you a man?" To minimize risks, they decided to dress well and to be polite at all costs, whatever the action taken against them. As they expected, they were not served when they sat down at the lunch counter on February 1, but neither were they arrested. When they walked back to the college, one of them recalled, they felt good: "At long last, we felt we had done something, not just talk about things."[10]

Theirs was a small action with big consequences. When other A&T students learned of it, they joined in, raising the expected anger of segregationists. To prepare themselves better, the students turned to the Congress of Racial Equality (CORE), which had conducted similar demonstrations in the north; CORE volunteers trained them in the techniques of nonviolent protest, establishing a pattern of student behavior for the next few years. Within weeks the news of what had happened at Greensboro precipitated an explosion of student sit-ins throughout the South. By the end of March 1960, demonstrations in at least 100 cities had involved more than 70,000 students and brought at least 3,600 arrests.

In Atlanta, one of the more liberal cities of the South, students from six black colleges issued a declaration: "Today's youth will not sit by submissively, while being denied all rights, privileges, and joys of life." Their sit-ins actively demanded the desegregation of the city's largest department store and, soon, of the entire downtown shopping district. In Nashville, Tennessee, John Hope II of Fisk University reported that "svelte co-eds from the sheltered homes of the affluent middle-class, with no apparent past interest in the problems of race, have shared their purpose and their suffering with their equally striking and poised sisters whose marches jeopardized their jobs, their scholarships and, thus, their priceless educational opportunities."[11] By 1961 the movement had spread from lunch counters to parks, swimming pools, theaters, churches, libraries, museums, and other public facilities, establishing the democratic doctrine of equality in the halls of ordinary life.

Almost from the beginning, black students received support from some of their white counterparts, and soon a growing number of young whites chose to follow the avenue of meaningful action that blacks had opened. From parents or from schools, they had absorbed a strong belief in liberal democratic ideals that the new movement now enabled them to practice. Rebelling against the political apathy of the 1950s, they organized to support the sit-ins. In the North, students groups provided financial aid to southern demonstrators and held their own demonstrations against segregation. They picketed the local stores of Woolworth's and other chains that practiced discrimination in their southern branches. One Columbia University student, when asked why he was picketing a store in Harlem, explained that until the sit-ins, he and his fellow students had wanted to protest against segregation, "but, aside from listening to speeches with which we agree—there was little to do."[12]

Undoubtedly, many student protesters took considerable pleasure in confuting the frequent complaints of their elders that they were passive, conformist, and lacking in idealism, and they were not reluctant to show up the parent generation for its failure to abide by its own ideals. Although most white students remained in the comparative safety of the North, a few journeyed south to share the risks of a direct confrontation with segregation, demonstrating their solidarity with black youth. Some were beaten up by segregationists, often brutally. In June 1961, for instance, the Associated Press reported the experience of Kenneth Shilman, an eighteen-year-old from New York: Shilman said that he and others had been arrested and then kept in a jail in their underwear with lights shining night and day, after electric cattle prods had been used on them. Shilman claimed to have seen two other young whites from Chicago being dragged naked down a jail corridor, their skin tearing on the rough concrete floor, when they refused to cooperate with their jailers. And in the same year a

Mississippi mob savagely beat two white northern student leaders, Paul Potter and Tom Hayden—a portent of other brutalities such as the murder of three young civil rights workers in 1964.

The majority of demonstrators of both races remained with the faith of their fathers, identifying with established civil rights organizations such as NAACP, but a significant minority declared their independence from the older generation, convinced that youth had found a new path to a new land. Less than six months after the first sit-ins, the black writer Louis Lomax predicted that they had opened a powerful new phase in the struggle against racism by shifting "the main issue to one of human dignity rather than civil rights." The students, said Lomax, had "set off an old-fashioned revival that has made integration an article of faith with the Negro masses who, like other masses, are apathetic toward voting and education."[13] The new mood was impatient with courtrooms and legal proceedings and with promises of equality in the distant future. Like the abolitionists of the previous century, they rejected gradualism in favor of immediate action, of now and not tomorrow. Instead of associating with old-line organizations, some student leaders decided in April 1960 to form their own operation, the Student Nonviolent Coordinating Committee (SNCC), which introduced a youthful idealism into the civil rights campaign. SNCC emphasized nonviolence not only as a tactical necessity but as the first step toward "a social order based on justice permeated with love." One of its members, James M. Lawson Jr., who had been expelled from the Vanderbilt Divinity School for civil rights activity, declared that the sit-ins were not "just a lot of nonsense over a hamburger," as some apparently believed, but a judgment upon "half-way efforts to deal with a radical social evil."[14] Beyond changes in the law to eliminate segregation, the young leaders dreamed of a truly brotherly society respectful of the human dignity as well as the fundamental equality of all Americans, regardless of color or background.

Their attitude and example significantly quickened the civil rights movement, and they set a pattern of radical social change for a growing number of students. On the other hand, though, they also threatened to divide the movement along generational lines. Especially among those who had experienced the barbarities of the segregationist South, activist youth developed a shared feeling that there was something radically wrong with American society, a radical wrong that their fathers and other adults had done nothing to eliminate. When adult society hesitated to act against evil, it, too, was condemned as evil. And so there appeared the idea of a generation gap between complacent older hypocrites and heroic youth, an idea that obscured the adult sources of the ideals that governed the young.

The new civil rights effort to complete the unfinished business of American democracy had a great impact on the thought and imagination of the new generation as it came of age. Among numerous other influences at work, however, the most significant involved one part of modern American society which had the surest claim and broadest influence on the developing young: the rapidly growing number of college and university students. It was within the halls of ivy that democracy's children launched their most ambitious effort to transform America along democratic lines.

NOTES

1. Duane Lockard, "American Subculture: The Negro Paradox," *Political Science Quarterly* 26 (1962): 257.

2. Robert Coles, "When I Draw the Lord He'll Be a Real Man," *Atlantic Monthly* 217 (1966): 75; E. Franklin Frazier, *Negro Youth at the Crossroads* (New York, 1967), 264.

3. Abram Kardiner and Lionel Ovesey, *The Mark of Oppression* (Cleveland, OH, 1962), 302, 310; Phyllis Harrison-Rose and Barbara Wyden, *The Black Child* (New York, 1973), 17, 28, 51–52, 112.

4. Miriam Goldberg, "Factors affecting Educational Attainments in Depressed Urban Areas," in A. Harry Passow, ed., *Education in Depressed Areas* (New York, 1963), 86.

5. Salisbury, *Shook-Up Generation*, 19.

6. Claude Brown, *Manchild in the Promised Land* (New York, 1965), 187–88.

7. Louis Wirth, "The Unfinished Business of American Democracy," *Annals of the American Academy of Political and Social Sciences* 244 (1946): 7; Mary Ellen Goodman, *Race Awakening in Your Child* (Cambridge, MA, 1952), 190–91.

8. Virgil A. Clift, "The Attack on Segregated Education Continues," *School and Society* 75 (1952): 361.

9. Gilbert Osofsky, ed. *The Burden of Race* (New York, 1967), 477; Albert Q. Maisel, "The Negroes among Us," *Reader's Digest* (September 1955): 106.

10. Charles U. Smith, "The Sit-Ins and the New Negro Student," in Ward Raab, ed., *American Race Relations Today* (Garden City, NY, 1962), 70–72; Louis E. Lomax, *The Negro Revolt* (New York, 1963), 133–36.

11. John Hope II, "The Negro College Student Protest and the Future," *Journal of Negro Education* 30 (1961): 370–71.

12. Osofsky, *Burden of Race*, 544–46; Lomax, *Negro Revolt*, 140–43.

13. Louis E. Lomax, "The Negro Revolt against Negro Leaders," *Harper's Magazine* 220 (June 1960): 41–48.

14. Quoted in Francis Broderick and August Meir, eds., *Negro Protest Thought in the Twentieth Century* (Indianapolis, IN, 1965), 275–80.

CHAPTER **Six**

NEW RADICALS, NEW HOPES

THE 1960S BROUGHT A STEADY RISE OF RADICAL THOUGHT AND behavior among a small but prominent portion of the maturing new generation, especially among college students. By the end of the decade, some of these young radicals would come to dream of a great purging revolution that would overthrow what they saw as a corrupt, bloodythirsty, fascist "Amerika."

The new radicalism of the 1960s erupted out of perhaps the most prosperous times known in human history. Although there had been some mild economic downturns since World War II, the baby-boom generation had known little but prosperity, an often noted but overrated difference between the young and their parents. Whereas older Americans had experienced the worst depression in history, the young had grown up in a time of great and steady progress. "Never before in all the world's history," declared one writer in 1957, "has any nation known such a flood tide of prosperity, nor one so long sustained."[1]

America seemed to have found the way to end the age-old curse of scarcity even after it had exhausted its geographical frontier. Through their effective organization of the economy, the great business corporations had created a well-ordered production system seemingly capable of delivering whatever the people wanted, and more. Through the increasing use of technology, they also promised to create growing leisure for all, an escape from the curse of excessive labor to the freedom to enjoy life's blessings. And through the expanded operations of the liberal welfare state, some measure of these blessings could also be brought to the poor and disadvantaged. In material plenty the American dream of freedom and happiness would eventually be realized for everyone.

That was the American Way. And it was one that the new generation seemed likely to sustain: "Babies are consumers from the moment of their birth," declared one observer. "The millions born during the war years are in high school now. In another five or six years they will be marrying and having babies of their own, creating vast new markets for houses, cars, and the myriad products of industry."[2]

The majority of the new generation satisfied this expectation. As they matured, most young Americans accepted the affluent society as at least a given, if not a good, and prepared themselves to join it. In 1959 a nationwide survey of some 10,000 college-bound high school graduates indicated that most of them fit comfortably into their parents' world, their greatest concerns being over jobs and families of their own. A follow-up study four years later found that most of them had pursued these goals in college and seemed satisfied with their life experiences. That majority, however, did not tell the whole story of a generation; a substantial minority had not felt the golden touch of affluence. As the economist John Kenneth Galbraith pointed out, prosperity had not eliminated the poor but only reduced them to a minority in most communities—a gain for society as a whole but no great blessing for the poverty-stricken, whose minority status left them with even less power to demand notice than before. In a society that took pride in its expanding middle class, the presence of poverty was something that could and, in the eyes of some, should be ignored.

By the early 1960s, though, the great attention given to juvenile delinquency and then, even more, the civil rights movement not only forced public notice of the matter but also made the poor even more aware of their exclusion from the affluent society. Among them were young people prepared to challenge the existing social order, at least until they too were admitted through the golden door. The poor, especially the black poor, became a central concern of the 1960s, if only because their possible alienation from society posed a standing danger to security and order.

The greatest challenge to the affluent society, however, came from some of those who had enjoyed its blessings, young members of the middle and upper-middle classes. Some, perhaps a great many, were affected by widespread concern over the moral softness in society, which led John F.

Kennedy to warn that Americans had neglected their "deeper values in favor of material strength. We have traveled in 100 years from the age of the pioneer to the age of payola." Material plenty seemed to bring social flabbiness. "Are we on the decline, a stagnant society," wondered one student, "or can we become visionaries again?" Some of the young were also influenced by complaints that the materially easy life had left them soft and uncaring. "The greatest danger," wrote one high school senior in 1961, "is not growing physically soft, but just rotting away because we get what we want so easily."[3] Such feelings were often fed by their parents' tales of triumphs over Depression adversities. In a society of plenty where their lives had been planned often through to the end of college, what challenge was there for the young people, what opportunity to prove to themselves and others that they could rise to a challenge, that they could be men and women?

Moreover, many young people who had come to expect that they could develop their talents and their personalities in the pursuit of some worthy goal found that both college and society seemed to demand that they conform to a system managed by their elders. The situation was especially hard on those whose interests were intellectual and idealistic. For them, the times had little to offer, since the 1950s—years of Cold War and nuclear terror, of conformity and consumerism—had been unkind to both ideas and ideals. In the universities, where they had hoped to find intellectual excitement, they often found an overspecialized scholarship devoted to matters obscure and, to them, irrelevant. Indeed, it seemed that affluence, despite pious hopes to the contrary, was threatening to stifle the thought and imagination that made life worth living.

By 1960, however, there were new hopes for a meaningful life. The sit-ins against segregation in the South offered a worthy role for youth as fighters against a cruel and archaic system of racism. Many young people, white as well as black, found in SNCC a romantic example of personal sacrifice for a noble cause. Another meaningful and less risky role was soon to be provided by the Peace Corps, which generated considerable excitement on the campuses even before its enactment by Congress in August 1961. Despite sneers at "Kennedy's Kiddie Corps," the new organization continued to attract the attention of the young and idealistic; during its first five years, more than 100,000 Americans applied for Peace Corps service, and some 14,000 actually served overseas in forty-eight countries. Here was one of the ways that they could respond to President Kennedy's call: "Ask not what your country can do for you; ask what you can do for your country."

Moreover, to satisfy their thirst for intellectual life, the young were discovering a well of new ideas that defied the stuffiness of the 1950s. In literature, they found, among others, Norman Mailer, who called their attention to such exotic affronts to conventionalism as the beatniks. In psychology, they encountered the sexual mysticism of Norman O. Brown, who raised their hopes that a better life lay beyond their uptight society. In social welfare, they found Michael Harrington, the young socialist who had called their attention to the existence of poverty in the midst of affluence even before the publication of his *Other America* in 1962. And they discovered a progressive critic of conventional schooling in Paul Goodman, who appreciated their need for significant involvement in a society that seemed organized largely to frustrate that need. An advocate of deliberately simple social forms scaled to human size, Goodman played the role of "utopian agent provocateur," as Harrington termed him, who inspired feelings of rebellion against an all too well-organized society.

Mailer, Brown, Harrington, and Goodman became heroes of the new culture with which the adventuresome and restless young eagerly identified, but none exercised more influence on the minds of young intellectuals than the sociologist C. Wright Mills. With his love of motorcycles and of the Wobblies—the Industrial Workers of the World, fearless American radicals of earlier days—Mills seemed to personify rebellion against conventionalism, and his sociological writings were acts of rebellion against orthodoxy in scholarship. Years before his death at age forty-six in 1962, he rejected the bland neutrality of his profession in favor of a biting criticism of the affluent society, which he believed was transforming once proudly independent Americans into "cheerful robots." His first major book, *White Collar* (1951), was scornful of the middle-class office worker who served the increasingly bureaucratic society and whom Mills characterized as "pushed by forces beyond his control, pulled into movements he does not understand, . . . the small creature who is acted upon."[4]

Having described the servants of the modern system, Mills proceeded in his best-known book, *The Power Elite* (1956), to describe the men whom the system had created to manage it—business leaders, labor leaders, and leading government bureaucrats whose willingness to cooperate with one another assured the dominance of the system: "Their high position is not the result of moral virtue; their fabulous success is not firmly connected with meritorious ability."[5] These leaders were not likely to have much respect for higher human values.

Mills spent the remaining years of his life in the attempt to rally Americans against what he believed was an immoral system of power. Convinced that the idea of scholarly objectivity was only a pretense for acceptance of the system, he turned to sociological polemics, driven by the hope that persons of ideas like himself could not only identify social ills but mobilize human beings to eliminate them. In the late 1950s he urged intellectuals and other thoughtful Americans to work against the current "deterioration of aspiration" by offering the public new visions of what might be in America. Like some others, he called for a revival of utopian thinking to break the stagnation of social imagination. With an animating vision of something radically new, even the remorseless power of systems could be overcome, and man could again be the maker rather than the victim of history: "These systems can be changed. Fate can be transcended."[6]

Mills offered a view of society that thoughtful and restless youth could appreciate. He gave them a target for their concerns: the impersonal and irresponsible authority of the System, a thing far different from the personal authority of parents and other individuals. And he gave them a way to deal with the problem. In 1960 he proposed a new radicalism to challenge the status quo. During the Cold War the old left-wing radicalism of Communists and Socialists had fallen apart, the victim not only of McCarthyism but of internal disillusionment and discord. Yet it was possible to create a New Left suited to contemporary conditions, one which, guided by a fresh eye, could discern the basic defects and sordid weaknesses in the foundations of what passed as contemporary social reality.

Apparently, the New Left was to reach back in time beyond Marxism to the older tradition of utopian speculation that Marxists had long scorned. Where the Old Left had attempted to attach its hopes to historical necessity, the New would seek the freedom of utopian thinkers to reinvent history. Mills saw himself, said one of his disciples, as "a political desperado whose most desperate struggle was against a very pervasive despair," against doubts that a force for change could be raised.[7] His call for a New Left, however, found a ready response on some college campuses. In 1959 a group of graduate students at the University of Wisconsin initiated *Studies on the Left*, a periodical devoted to reviving radical thought in America. In the first issue its editors followed Mills in rejecting "objectivity" as the resort of those who were "browbeaten by things as they are" and in urging a scholarship devoted to the reconstruction of society on better foundations.[8] *Studies on the Left* was soon followed by other radical periodicals such as *New University Thought* at the University of Chicago and *The Activist* at Oberlin, a college which itself had been the product of an earlier, pre–Civil War radicalism. These journals became outlets for a small but determined band of student intellectuals excited by the adventure of radicalism and directed by democratic ideals. For many of these young people, whose intellectual maturity had left them outside high school peer-group society, the New Left provided a welcomed sense of community and a belief that they had found a worthy channel for their talents.

The young radical students might have been content to remain in the world of ideas, but the times were such as to encourage and demand action. The sit-ins of black students against the racist system of the South was a challenge to young white radicals to mount a campaign of their own. The formation of SNCC was soon followed by the formation of the premier white radical organization of the 1960s, Students for a Democratic Society (SDS). It began as the student branch of the League for Industrial Democracy, a socialist organization which itself was descended from the Intercollegiate Socialist Society founded in 1905 by Jack London and Upton Sinclair. Originating at the University of Michigan, SDS soon established strong chapters at Swarthmore College in Pennsylvania, the University of Texas, Johns Hopkins, and Harvard. In 1965 it declared its independence from the League for Industrial Democracy in order to pursue a course of radical activism free from the cautiousness of the parent organization.

The founders of SDS were pre–baby boom people such as the originator of the organization's idea, Robert Alan (Al) Haber, who was born in 1936, the son of a New Deal liberal. They were old enough to have been influenced directly by the democratic liberalism of the World War II era and yet also young enough to be part of the new generation. Typical in some respects but also significantly untypical was the one among them destined to achieve the greatest influence and fame, Thomas Emmett Hayden (born 1939). Tom Hayden was an exception in that he was born a Roman Catholic, a faith that produced very few radicals; his conservative father did not speak to him for years during the sixties. The probability that he was named after a prominent Irish rebel, Thomas Addis Emmett, suggests that some radicalism existed in his background, however. As a student at the University of Michigan in the late 1950s, Hayden became a prominent dissenter, editing the *Michigan Daily* into one of the foremost student newspapers in the country and then founding VOICE, a student political party. After he graduated from the university in 1961, he remained there to write his master's thesis on C. Wright Mills, with whom he shared a love for motorcycles as well as for radical ideas.

Tom Hayden helped set a pattern for many of those student radicals who were hungry for some kind of social action to authenticate their idealism. Responding to the example of SNCC, whose members he called a "courageous moral vanguard," he chose in 1961 to venture into the South to work for the cause of human rights, impelled, as he said later, by the desire not only to participate in the making of history but also to make a personally validating commitment, one that involved "defining not only yourself but also your life by risking your life, and testing whether you're willing to die for your beliefs." At McComb, Mississippi, in October, he confronted his test, being beaten up by segregationists along with Paul Potter, a student at Swarthmore and soon to be a leader of SDS. Hayden, however, recognized that what he called a "noble morality" was not enough; it was necessary to work toward an understanding of essential social problems and of fundamental social alternatives. Borrowing from the progressivism of the educator John Dewey, he defined radicalism as a constant striving for social answers freed from the restraints of dogmatism, Marxist and otherwise: "Answers are seen as provisional, to be discarded in the face of new evidence or changed conditions."[9]

Hayden soon made a significant contribution to American radical thought, being chiefly responsible for creating a manifesto for SDS, the *Port Huron Statement*, a seminal document of the new radicalism. Adopted by the first SDS national convention at Port Huron, Michigan, in June 1962, the *Port Huron Statement* was—probably by design—the American equivalent of the *Communist Manifesto*. It was a New World manifesto expressive of the hopes and frustrations of a new generation of radicals reared on American democratic traditions. Where the old manifesto had begun grimly with "A specter is haunting Europe—the specter of communism," the new began, "We are people of this generation, bred in at least modest comfort, housed in universities looking uncomfortably to the world we inherit." It first depicted the ideal nation in which the postwar young had believed they were growing up—an America not only wealthy and powerful but devoted to freedom, equality, and world peace—in order to emphasize the deeply disappointing reality of a nation devoting itself to a worldwide Cold War at the expense of freedom at home and abroad.[10]

Much of the *Port Huron Statement* was directed toward disclosing fundamental national defects: a political and economic order managed by irresponsible corporate wealth, a society riven by poverty and by racial discrimination, and a foreign policy dominated by a "warfare state" driven to recklessness by an irrational fear of communism. Essentially, however, the statement was positive and hopeful. It set down its basic ideal for American democracy, of a society that recognized the "potential for self-cultivation, self-direction, self-understanding, and creativity" in all people, where the free striving of every person to realize his or her potential was balanced by a dedication to the welfare of others, where individualism was joined to brotherhood.[11] In place of what radicals saw as the establishment of the few reigning over the apathetic many, it called for the creation of a "participatory democracy," organized to encourage independence in all people and to provide the means for their participation in all decisions affecting their lives. Although the statement presented a long list of concrete proposals for fundamental change, it was this vision of a participatory democracy of freely active equals which best incorporated the hopes of the young radicals. It was the ideal of the democratic family given a social form.

The leaders of SDS anticipated a long campaign. They envisioned a New Left movement of university students and faculty members which would reach out from its campus stronghold to encourage and direct labor, civil rights, peace, and other liberal forces in society, the first aims being to win control of the Democratic Party and to retrieve America's traditions from their corrupting associations with southern racism, corporate business, bureaucracy, and Cold War policies. By restoring American democracy at home, they believed, they could make democratic America once again a model for the world and an influence for worldwide freedom and prosperity, a nation freed from the stultifying anticommunism of the Cold War, which in a nuclear world threatened disaster for the human race. Their manifesto ended with a mission declaration: "As students for a democratic society, we are committed to stimulating this kind of social movement, this kind of vision and program in campus and community across the country. If we appear to seek the unattainable, as it has been said, then let it be known that we do so to avoid the unimaginable."[12]

The founding of SDS was a notable act of youthful audacity. Convinced that past ideologies of the left as well as the right had little to say about the current situation, Hayden and the other founders rejected the old red compass of communism in favor of new directions often yet to be discovered. Convinced that the Old Left was irrelevant, they largely ignored the organizations that had dominated radicalism in America over the previous half-century. Convinced that the liberalism of the Democratic Party was the corrupted liberalism of a conservative establishment, they broke with that party and its powerful allies, even rejecting the New Frontier of youthful John F. Kennedy as not new enough.

They had no great strength in numbers: in 1963, the total SDS membership was about 1,000 organized in some twenty campus chapters, a minuscule portion of a student population numbering millions and a tiny showing against the hundreds of thousands enrolled in thousands of college fraternities and sororities. Yet there was strength beyond numbers. The majority of SDS members were a special breed from a special tradition. According to Richard Flacks, who was both a leader of SDS and a student of its affairs, its members came largely from middle- and upper-middle-class families that were mostly Jewish or liberal Protestant, backgrounds that had provided a disproportionate share of American radicals and reformers in the past. Some were "red-diaper babies," the sons and daughters of Communists and Socialists, but more important, most came from the broader tradition of progressive liberalism that stretched back to the World War II period. They were the ones most likely to have been exposed to a democratic, child-centered upbringing, to progressive education, and to habits of social involvement.

Although in one respect they rejected their parents' past, in another they had their feet firmly planted in a directly meaningful past of progressive reform that included their parents. Although like other students they often acted out of personal discontents, what distinguished them was the sense of social commitment inherited from that past. Coming from well-educated families where they had been encouraged to express their own thoughts, they were unusually articulate, producing a highly disproportionate number of student orators, writers, and editors. And as a potential public, they could look to younger students like themselves—a minority of activists in a desert of student apathy but significant because the new generation was so large.

Besides placing their hopes in the expanding youth population, early SDS members looked outside the university for a constituency. Unlike the Old Left, they had little faith in the working class, which had so often disappointed radicals, but SNCC and the civil rights campaign called their attention to the possibility that the poor and disadvantaged—the hitherto ignored—could be organized into a force for radical change. In 1963, Tom Hayden and Carl Wittman, another SDS member, gave serious attention to the idea of creating an interracial movement of the poor, one that would include not only poor whites as well as blacks but Mexicans, Puerto Ricans, and other new minorities. They were not particularly hopeful about the willingness of white ethnics to forgo their hostility toward blacks, but they treated such a coalition as the key to their hopes for radical change, warning that without it, poor blacks and poor whites would continue to struggle against each other instead of against the power structure. This idea was to play a critical role in the history of SDS throughout the sixties.

As Hayden and other leaders saw the situation, the first step toward implementing the idea was to draw the poor out of their traditional apathy. SNCC had begun to work toward this end among the poor blacks of the South. In line with its own dream of participatory democracy, SDS set out to organize the poor of northern cities in the belief that they were potentially the most reliably radical constituency to be found in America. In the summer of 1963, SDS created the Economic Research and Action Project (ERAP)—funded by a $5,000 grant from the liberal United Auto Workers union—to develop a strategy for the poor. By the end of the year, persuaded by the example of SNCC, SDS shifted the emphasis in the project from research to action, and a number of members spread out to work as full-time community organizers in the slums of Chicago, Cleveland, Baltimore, and Newark.

Over the next years, these back-to-the-people projects experienced varying degrees of failure. In Cleveland, twelve young men and women formed a collective household (where, in equality, men assumed an equal share of the cooking and cleaning) to allow them time for community organizing. They tried to create organizations for the unemployed, for tenants, and for people on welfare, each intended to exert some pressure on the people who controlled the lives of the poor. Their tenants' council had some success in pressuring landlords to improve living conditions in their buildings, but the effort was soon quashed by local authorities, who scared the poor tenants off. Everywhere, the would-be reformers struggled unsuccessfully to overcome a pervasive pattern of apathy, cynicism, suspicion, and ignorance. In Chicago an attempt to organize the unemployed had a similarly limited success, the chief result being the discovery that the poor were inclined to blame their plight not on the System but on either themselves or on blacks, women, and other people who they believed had taken their jobs.

The most promising ERAP project was in Newark, New Jersey, where Tom Hayden determined to settle after he had completed his thesis on C. Wright Mills. He and his SDS colleagues moved into a black ghetto area, the Clinton Hill section, where they formed the Newark Community Union, comprising various local organizations each of which was intended to represent the people on a particular block. Convinced that the established leadership, both black and white, had consistently betrayed the interests of the poor and powerless, they attempted to develop a working model of participatory democracy: "We don't believe in leadership. We believe in one man, one vote. . . . We discuss each problem that occurs on our blocks and let the people decide what kind of action they want to take to solve the problem."[13]

After more than a year of exhausting work by the organizers, the Newark Community Union could claim some small success, having generated pressures leading to repairs in some rundown tenements and to improved garbage collection; it also contributed to the defeat of an urban renewal project that had threatened to uproot thousands of the poor. There as elsewhere, however, it proved very difficult to overcome general apathy. Moreover, SDS discovered that it could count on very few student recruits to sustain, much less expand, such efforts, the campaign against racism having attracted most of the committed. At the end of 1964 it terminated the national project.

So ended the most significant experiment in participatory democracy. In large part, the experiment became the victim of a change in direction within the student movement that would significantly alter the character and membership of SDS. As had been true of earlier efforts, the change grew out of the southern civil rights movement, which had consistently overshadowed the northern project. During the 1960s the southern movement experienced periods of despair as well as hope. After a trip to the South the editor of *The Activist* at Oberlin College wrote that not only were young white southerners seemingly the most prejudiced age group, but many young southern black students hung back from the cause. At some of the black colleges, he wrote, "instead of student rallies, fund raising, and sit-ins, one finds campus elections determining who the next college queen will be for homecoming."[14] But civil rights leaders pressed on. By 1963, SNCC was becoming increasingly more determined and more radical in response to what it saw as the reluctance of the Kennedy administration to move rapidly against segregation in the South, and it began to recruit northern college students to participate in the assault on segregation.

Much of its effort was concentrated in Mississippi, the keystone state of segregation and a source of much violence against civil rights workers; in 1963, a black civil rights leader, Medgar Evers, had been murdered there. The response in 1963 was enough to encourage SNCC to plan for an even larger campaign in the summer of 1964. More than 500 students were selected from a much larger number of volunteers and trained to participate in voter registration drives or to teach in the "freedom schools" established by SNCC to cope with widespread illiteracy among Mississippi blacks. These were their ways of challenging the basis of white racist power.

Participating in the "freedom summer" of 1964 was like participating in a war. Three young civil rights workers, James Chaney, Andrew Goodman, and Michael Schwerner, were murdered; at least two others were shot at, six beaten, and some 200 arrested. Nevertheless, it was a heroic and meaningful campaign that brought results, since, along with similar campaigns elsewhere, it finally broke the back of segregation in the South after more than a decade of attack. For participants, such an effort had significant personal benefits. It assuaged the guilt of those students who were uncomfortable with their advantaged status, and it was a proving ground for those who wished to test their personal courage and commitment. Above all, it was that something worthy to do, which many students had hungered for. Most probably agreed with the young San Francisco State College student who, after several years of supporting civil rights from afar, ventured south into Georgia to confront segregation head-on: "We were Americans at last; we weren't really afraid—shaking and defecating in our pants, yes, but afraid, no; we were in the field, working for the ideals . . . [of] equality, justice, freedom. And we were side by side with other Americans: all those beautiful black people who had faced fear and through it had become strong. They imbued us with a new patriotism, a new vision of the American dream."[15]

If they returned to campus with a new patriotism and a new vision, however, these students also brought a grimmer view of an America of indifference and violence, which generally left them suspicious of authority—including that of their own universities. This civil rights activism was the critical element in the explosion of student discontent in late 1964 at the Berkeley campus of the University of California, an event that marked the beginning of a distinctly new phase in the student movement.

Berkeley was the natural place for such an explosion to take place. Along with other Bay area universities, it was a primary recruiting ground for civil rights activism, in part because it had independently evolved its own tradition of student radicalism: in 1960, Berkeley students had demonstrated against the red-baiting HUAC, an action that ended in an attack by the local police on the student protesters. Moreover, the university had been the first to produce an independent student party, SLATE, dedicated to ending the era of sandbox student government. Although SLATE was unable to win a campus majority, it did rally students in support of changes in university policy, including the abolition of compulsory Reserve Officers' Training Corps (ROTC) courses, a bit of Cold War militarism that was becoming increasingly unpopular on many campuses. From its large student body, Berkeley was able to provide members for various other activist organizations such as Students for Civil Liberties and Utopians for Political Action, making its campus the liveliest in the nation.

Whatever their particular mission, these student groups shared a common suspicion of the university administration, headed by Clark Kerr, the leading proponent of the multiversity. As president of the University of California system, Kerr had succeeded in making the Berkeley campus a major research center, a significant part of the knowledge industry, which pleased many faculty members as well as the business community and the defense industry. Although most Berkeley students were satisfied with their experience, others were unhappy with what they saw as the impersonality and pressures of an educational factory. Many of the discontented responded by dropping out, some to transfer to other universities and others to join a bohemian community that had grown up near the campus and become one of the seedbeds for the soon-to-appear hippie movement. Student activists generally, however, remained to fight the system. In 1962, three members of SLATE published a criticism of Kerr's philosophy in the radical press. They charged that Kerr was primarily interested in training students to fit into some specialized niche in the industrial system—a far cry from their ideal of a university "as a community of scholars bound together by the search for truth and feeling a responsibility to their society."[16] Although some of their discontent was directed at the university curriculum, the chief cause of resentment involved the university's relationship with society at large, which activists came to see as a threat to their freedom.

The basic issue, like so much else, developed out of the civil rights movement. In late 1963, Berkeley students began a series of demonstrations against racial discrimination, picketing various local businesses, including the *Oakland Tribune*. By March, more than 150 student demonstrators had been arrested. The demonstrations antagonized some powerful interests at a time when the university was trying to rally support behind an important bond issue for higher education, making it especially vulnerable to outside demands that it rein in the activists. Soon, the controversy focused on the nerve center of student activism, the "Bancroft Strip" at the Telegraph Avenue entrance to the campus, where students had customarily set up tables with literature and petitions relating to their various causes. The strip was the university's Hyde Park corner of unlimited free speech and a place of recruitment for various demonstrations like the ones against discrimination. In September 1964 the Berkeley administration attempted to placate the business community by limiting this freedom.

The decision antagonized student organizations of all persuasions. When five students were cited for using the strip in violation of the new rules, 500 others appeared with them at the dean's office; and when the dean refused to drop the charges, they began a sit-in of Sproul Hall. Although the university leaned toward reversing its unpopular decision, it made the mistake of trying to punish some of the demonstrators, producing even more student discontent. Soon, the dissenters organized the Free Speech Movement (FSM), and found a spokesman in Mario Savio, a twenty-two-year-old student recently returned from a perilous participation in SNCC's Mississippi freedom summer.

Like the members of SNCC, Savio distrusted any leadership, even his own, but he was willing to voice what he thought were student discontents. In one speech he told students that they faced a common threat to democracy: "In Mississippi, an autocratic and powerful minority rules. . . . In California, the privileged minority manipulates the University to suppress the students' political expression." The freedom of student activists, he said, was of great importance to the whole nation: "The most exciting things going on in America today are movements to change America. America is becoming ever more the utopia of sterilized, outmoded contentment."[17]

The affair reached a climax in December, beginning with a call from FSM for another sit-in. Some 6,000 young people gathered for a mass rally in support of the protest. After listening to Joan Baez, the popular folk singer, sing the new youth anthem "Blowin' in the Wind" ("How many roads must a man walk down / Before you call him a man"), they heard Savio urge them to bring the university to a stop: "You've got to put your bodies on the gears and upon the wheels."[18] Then 800 protesters occupied Sproul Hall. The university responded by calling in the police, who cleared the hall, sometimes with brutal force: they were seen dragging one girl student feet-first down a flight of stairs, her head hitting each of the ninety steps. And there were mass arrests. So much for *in loco parentis* at Berkeley. The authorities won this battle but lost the war, for the student response was to initiate a strike that brought the university machine to a stop. Confronted with an organized rebellion within and much criticism from without, the administration capitulated in early 1965 and restored the customary student right to free speech and the use of the Bancroft Strip.

Having protected student freedoms, FSM largely disbanded, but it experienced a brief rebirth followed by a permanent demise over a rather farcical but also ominous incident. In March 1965 a nonstudent appeared on campus with a sign displaying the word "fuck." His intention seems to have been to call attention to the hypocritical morality of a society that condemned a word related to procreation while using with disturbing frequency another four-letter word, "kill." When he was promptly arrested, some students reacted by rallying in favor of the right to use obscenities as part of free speech, and FSM reluctantly entered the dispute on the same side. It was an unfortunate affair, since it enabled critics to label FSM the "Filthy Speech Movement," thereby downgrading its importance as a defender of student free speech for significant causes.

Probably no nonathletic event in the history of American universities attracted as much public attention and evoked as much discussion as the conflict at Berkeley. There had been many campus protests and riots elsewhere in previous years. In 1959, 1,000 or so Yale students had rioted in the streets of New Haven after someone threw a snowball! Three years later the students of the all-white University of Mississippi rioted against the admission of a black student, James Meredith. The Berkeley affair was different in that students there fought and won a battle with a powerful university over an important issue of human rights. It was a sign of the new maturity of students, no longer adolescents subject to an authority *in loco parentis* but young adults who demanded the power to run their own lives. Student power had exerted itself in defense of the right of students to support outside causes.

Berkeley tended to dominate the nation's headlines, but it was not the only or even the first university to experience conflict over free speech issues. In 1963, at Indiana University in Bloomington, students who sponsored the appearance of a black socialist on campus were charged by a county prosecutor with violating Indiana's Anti-Communist Act. There, however, they received the strong support of the university administration as well as of fellow students, avoiding the kind of conflict that developed at Berkeley. When the Indiana Civil Liberties Union was unable to handle the case, the protesters got the assistance of the radical Emergency Civil Liberties Committee in New York, which sent the lawyer Leonard Boudin to represent them. In 1964 he was able to persuade a local court to rule in the students' favor and against the state Anti-Communist Act.

Boudin himself had fathered a radical student: his daughter Kathy was to play a notorious role in the later history of SDS.

There were similar incidents elsewhere, often involving heavy-handed university administrations. At Michigan State University, for instance, the Young Socialists Club encountered the determined opposition of the university president, John Hannah, when it invited a known Communist to speak on campus. Such cases caused nationwide concern, and in the spring of 1965, representatives from thirty-nine colleges met to discuss "Democracy on Campus." After considerable debate, they adopted a students' bill of rights calling for freedom of assembly and of speech, student control over campus law enforcement, abolition of ROTC and of loyalty oaths, and joint student-faculty curriculum control. Before they adjourned, the delegates also adopted a resolution condemning universities as servants of the Establishment, an idea that was developing a powerful grip on young radicals.

By the mid-1960s, some student radicals had begun to graduate from their universities and to consider new ways of applying their experiences in a larger social context. Those who had acquired journalistic experience, especially on college newspapers, began to form what was soon called the underground press. Convinced that existing journalism was enslaved to the Establishment, they created their own newspapers, especially in major university towns. In 1964 a group founded the *Los Angeles Free Press*, and this was soon followed by similar newspapers in Berkeley, San Francisco, East Lansing, and New York City. By 1969, at their height, there were some 500 papers with more than a million readers.

Often supported by cooperatives that served as sustaining communities for the young journalists, these papers developed distinctive characters. The *San Francisco Oracle* so heavily reflected the drug-oriented culture of the area that it was widely believed to be associated with drug dealers. Detroit's *Fifth Estate*, concentrating on working-class issues, eventually denounced the existing labor unions as tools of the oppressive Establishment. Even the South gave birth to a few radical papers, notably Atlanta's *Great Speckled Bird* and, in the very heart of southern racism, *The Kudzu* of Jackson, Mississippi. Founded by David Doggett, the Mississippi-born and -educated son of a liberal Methodist minister, *Kudzu*'s open identification with civil rights and radicalism earned it the special enmity of the local police and made it one of the most persecuted papers in America. By challenging what they believed were the distortions promulgated by the Establishment press, the young journalists hoped to excite a popular awakening that would produce radical improvements in society and politics. One of the editors recalled that by 1967, when there were some twenty papers, "a shared vision of political and social rebellion began to focus," one that radicals hoped would eventually lead to a new democratic reality.[19]

All in all, it did seem by the middle of the 1960s that democracy's children were on the march toward a more democratic society. In 1965, one of the leaders of FSM at Berkeley declared that the movement had achieved a victory not only for student rights but for a more general reinvigoration of the democratic way: "It's a question of people getting into motion and acting and breaking rules and standing up to authority." Democracy, he believed, should involve all the people, but almost by default, another notion had established itself which threatened to shut the people out of the process: "It's become fashionable of late to talk about democratic politics in terms of elites, bargaining with each other."[20] Nevertheless, activism like the protests at Berkeley and in the South was a way whereby people could directly influence policy and effect change. And it seemed to be working, since there was a popular awakening to democracy led by the young in alliance with reform-minded people of all ages. Despite numerous setbacks—including the assassination of President John F. Kennedy—the first half of the 1960s had been good for democracy's children.

The movement toward a new democracy also found its own music to march by, music that embodied its radicalism and its hopeful view of America. Early in the decade, many college students turned from the popular music of their adolescence to folk music, reviving a musical form that had been a vehicle of protest at least since the days of the abolitionists. In the twentieth century the Wobblies had created a substantial body of labor protest songs, and the tradition had been carried into the 1940s by Woody Guthrie and Pete Seeger. The McCarthyism of the early 1950s threatened to extinguish the radical folk tradition; Pete Seeger and his group, the Weavers, were blacklisted for most of the decade, but this fact undoubtedly contributed to the appeal of folk music for the new generation of young radicals. In more basic ways, the young were attracted to the music because, although new to them, it seemed rooted in an earlier, more authentic America than the America of "power elites" and "organization men." Moreover, it blended well with the so-called Negro folk music that was playing its part in the civil rights movement in the South. And it was music not only to listen to but to participate in, the proper stuff of both communal singing and personal guitar picking (in 1963, it was estimated that some 6 million Americans, mostly young, were strumming—or at least owning—guitars). It was the music of participatory democracy.

The folk revival soon developed its own star performers and writers. Mary Travers, who had studied guitar with Pete Seeger in the 1950s, teamed up with two other folk singers to form the group Peter, Paul, and Mary; they made their version of an Old Left song, "If I Had a Hammer," one of the top songs of 1962. Even more closely identified with radicalism was Joan Baez (born in 1941), whose Mexican-Scottish heritage included a strong dash of radical Protestantism; her father, a physics professor, refused to have anything to do with war or the weapons of war, and her mother twice was jailed for her antiwar protests. Baez involved herself as well as her music in virtually every phase of the radical movement, demonstrating against segregation in the South and against war, and joining the FSM sit-in at Berkeley. In 1965 she founded the Institute for the Study of Nonviolence to promote peaceful change.

Baez's sometime associate Bob Dylan was distinctly less politically involved but even more musically significant. An admirer of Woody Guthrie, Dylan had worked his way up through beatnik coffeehouses to national fame as a performer and, even more, as a composer. Among the more than 200 songs that he wrote during the early sixties, "Blowin' in the Wind" became a civil rights anthem and "A Hard Rain's A-Gonna Fall" a powerful statement against the nuclear bomb. Dylan, however, was more poet than protester, and by the mid-1960s he had begun to turn his music inward, identifying his talents with the drug-oriented hippie culture that had sprung up in the major cities. The change won him even greater acclaim. "This thin youth with three harmonicas, a guitar and a heart full of poetry," wrote one young admirer, "has obviously tapped a great well of discontent, frustration, and yearning."[21] And so he had.

Dylan's conversion coincided with a disturbing new phase in the history of the new generation. Times were changing, but not for the better. The years 1964 and 1965 were the last truly positive years. The election of Lyndon Johnson over Barry Goldwater in November 1964 brought new hope not only to the cause of civil rights but to peace as well. Even SDS, with its suspicion of politicians, was prepared to "go part of the way with LBJ," and in 1964 some three-quarters of young Americans had a favorable view of the president.[22] And indeed, in the year after his election, Johnson strengthened civil rights and launched his ambitious War on Poverty, which satisfied radicals, often incorporating some of their ideas. In 1965, however, the president decided to expand what had been a limited American military involvement in a distant and still largely unknown Vietnam. By escalating what soon became a bloody foreign war, the Johnson administration antagonized a growing part of the new generation and helped create an atmosphere of hostility not only between generations but also among the young themselves. The hopeful, positive years were over.

NOTES

1. Harold M. Martin, "Can We Stay Rich?" *Saturday Evening Post* (July 13, 1957): 22; (July 27, 1957): 30.

2. Ibid. (July 27, 1957), 80.

3. "By Comfort Possessed," *Senior Scholastic* (September 20, 1961): 21; Otto Butz, *To Make a Difference: A Student Look at America* (New York, 1967), 121.

4. C. Wright Mills, *White Collar: The American Middle Class* (New York, 1951), xii–xviii.

5. C. Wright Mills, *The Power Elite* (New York, 1956), 361.

6. C. Wright Mills, *The Causes of World War III* (New York, 1958), 93, 140–41.

7. Carl Oglesby, ed., *The New Left Reader* (New York, 1969), 7–8.

8. James Weinstein and David W. Eakins, eds., *For a New America* (New York, 1970), 6–8.

9. Thomas Hayden, "A Letter to the New (Young) Left," in Mitchell Cohen and Dennis Hale, eds., *The New Student Left* (Boston, 1968), 6–7.

10. Paul Jacobs and Saul Landau, *The New Radicals: A Report with Documents* (New York, 1966), 149–50.

11. Ibid., 151–60.

12. Ibid., 157–58.

13. James Miller, *Democracy Is in the Streets: From Port Huron to the Siege of Chicago* (New York, 1987), 262–63; Jacobs and Landau, *New Radicals*, 174.

14. Cohen and Hale, *New Student Left*, 94–95.

15. Butz, *To Make a Difference*, 115–16.

16. Bruce Payne et al., "Theodicy of 1964: The Philosophy of Clark Kerr," in Cohen and Hale, *New Student Left*, 231.

17. Quoted in Jacobs and Landau, *New Radicals*, 230–34; and Hal Draper, *Berkeley: The New Student Revolt* (New York, 1965), 23–27.

18. Milton Viorst, *Fire in the Streets: America in the 1960s* (New York, 1979), 295.

19. Draper, *Berkeley*, 14.

20. Laurence Leamer, *The Paper Revolutionaries: The Rise of the Underground Press* (New York, 1972), 25–32; Kenneth Wachsberger, ed., *Voices from the Underground*, xvii–xix, 219–20.

21. Draper, *Berkeley*, 222.

22. Butz, *To Make a Difference*, 164.

CHAPTER **Seven**

YOUNG AMERICA AT WAR

THE GREAT MAJORITY OF THE FORTIES GENERATION WAS REACH-
ing maturity in the middle and late 1960s, a time that saw America
move from day into night. They had lived their late teens during a
period of general optimism and hope for a better future. The early 1960s
had their share of darkness—the Cuban missile crisis, the brutal attacks
on civil rights workers, and the assassination of President John F.
Kennedy—but they were also years when the evils of McCarthyism, the
Cold War, and racial segregation were significantly diminished. Even young
radicals could believe in the possibility of peaceful changes in the social
order. And they were also prosperous years, a time of opportunity especially for the young. In 1964 and 1965, reports were that good jobs awaited
college graduates, not only white men but women and African Americans
as well. Such were the opportunities that the idealistic young often deferred job offers in business for more personally meaningful roles in the
Peace Corps and other socially oriented occupations. Idealism was a rewarding adventure.

The mid-sixties, however, brought growing signs of restlessness and
discontent. In 1964, Fred M. Hechinger, the *New York Times* education
columnist, said that in the previous few years, colleges had reported a
steady improvement in the quality of students but also increases in
emotional problems and personal dissatisfaction, a major source of the

counterculture movement soon to erupt. And by the end of the decade the public climate had become a darkness of confusion and conflict. Although the solid majority of people continued with life as usual, a significant minority of America's best and brightest youth had exchanged hopes of peaceful change for bitter thoughts of revolution or had decided to abandon society entirely. In the streets and on the campuses, some of the young resorted to violence against society and against the law, a rejection of public authority unprecedented in American history.

What had happened? Conservatives often blamed the trouble on the character of the young malcontents. They were, in this view, the spoiled prodigies of permissive upbringing and self-indulgent affluence who selfishly refused to accept the ordinary constraints and obligations of social life. Others noted the sheer size of the new generation and the inevitable frictions and frustrations it faced in finding a satisfactory place in society. Whatever the attitudes and dispositions of youth, however, few doubted that the trouble owed much to changes in objective circumstances that threatened both the public hopes and private ambitions of many of the young, challenging their faith in the democratic system. Undoubtedly, the greatest threat came from America's rapidly growing military involvement in Vietnam. In early 1965, when President Johnson decided to escalate what had been a limited conflict on the other side of the world, he set in motion a series of developments that tarnished America's international image, disrupted domestic progress, and troubled the lives of millions of young Americans.

The war affected young men and women in many different ways. Of the some 53 million Americans who turned nineteen years of age during the seven years of conflict between 1964 and 1973, more than 8 million served in the military, more than 2 million in Vietnam. Of these, some 51,000 died and 270,000 were wounded. Americans over twenty-five constituted another 15 percent of the casualties. The risks of war were distributed unevenly among the young. The poor were more likely to see combat than the advantaged, southerners more than northerners, rural youth more than city boys. By 1969 the little town of Beallsville, Ohio, population 450, had lost five of its young men, killed in a part of the world that few had even known existed a few years before. In contrast, only two of the 1,200-member class of 1970 at Harvard University were known to have even gone to Vietnam. One study of Chicago indicated that men in poor neighborhoods were three times as likely to die in the war as those from advantaged areas. Yet even those who did not serve were often also profoundly affected by the war.

The conflict served to deepen differences among American youth. At one extreme it received the support of the often unnoticed young people whose conservatism led them to support any war against communism as an act of national patriotism. Generally overlooked in the public notice given to radical students were uncounted numbers who had been educated to fight the Cold War. Throughout the decade the National Education Center at Harding College in Searcy, Arkansas, served as an intellectual hub for a right-wing movement that combined religious fundamentalism and political conservatism into a crusade against communism. In other areas, right-wing businessmen funded "Teens against Communism" groups to fight supposed leftist influences in the public schools, including the influence of progressive education, which was denounced as "Red-ucation."[1]

How many young people were actually recruited to this cause is unknown, but it undoubtedly contributed to the development of the religious conservatism that affected the next decades. Easier to count was the minority of college students who belonged to conservative organizations, particularly YAF, which, at least one study indicated, drew on families of a lower social standing than did SDS. Whereas the strength of the left was in the major universities, the right had its special place in small church-related colleges. In 1965 the 25,000-member YAF met in its annual convention and adopted resolutions calling for the escalation of the Vietnam War—and also for the right of fraternities to practice discrimination in their membership policies. In that year, YAF also launched a recruitment campaign and by 1970 had doubled its membership.

Support for the war, however, was not limited to the right. The conflict, after all, had been initiated and sustained by Democratic presidents committed to liberal causes. Aside from a great many apathetics who took no position, the majority who took a stand on the war supported it in the hope that it would accomplish its official goals of defeating communism and establishing democracy in Southeast Asia. Especially in church-related colleges and in the regional universities, where students from middle-class families of limited income and education predominated, there was little disposition to question the national government's foreign-policy decisions. As late as May 1967, when college students were asked to identify themselves as either "hawks" or "doves," the score was hawks, 49 percent; doves, 35 percent. Opposition to the war was greatest where student activism was greatest, in the major universities, but even there, antiwar students were in the minority at least in the beginning. In late 1965, it was reported that at Berkeley they constituted only 25 percent of the student body. Another study found that no more than 2 percent of students overall were politically active: "The overwhelming majority of American college students are politically apathetic—caught up in vocational, academic, or hedonistic pursuits."[2]

The majority, however, was passive in its acceptance, whereas the antiwar dissenting minority had both the disposition and the experience to carry on an aggressive campaign. Often young leaders of influence on campus, they had the support of the NSA, which in 1965 at its annual meeting in Madison, Wisconsin, called for an end to offensive military action in Vietnam. This was the work of a 100-member Liberal Caucus that represented SDS and SNCC along with various other protest groups; most of its members had worked for civil rights. Over the next years, these groups were able to recruit substantial numbers of other students.

Antiwar leaders found two fundamental issues around which to rally student opposition. One issue involved the essential character of the war. Especially for those students who had been educated to question all authority, it was easy to dispute official pronouncements that the aim of the conflict was to advance freedom. They concluded that to the contrary, their country had begun an unjust war of aggression against a people seeking their independence from foreign oppression. How could one support a policy, wrote one student, "in which under the banner of self-determination and democracy, my country invades a foreign land, interferes in a civil war, sets up puppet governments, bombs hospitals, schools and whole villages of people who never heard of democracy, burns children with jellied gasoline, and refuses to hold promised elections?" And they saw the war was doubly unjust, since it demanded the sacrifice of money and attention needed to resolve important problems at home: ending racial discrimination, eliminating poverty, and establishing equality for all the people. "The war in Vietnam," declared SDS in early 1965, "injures both Vietnamese and Americans and should be stopped."[3]

The forties generation was not the first to confront a questionable war—the Mexican War of the 1840s had also been denounced as an unjust act of aggression—but its members were the first to face the prospect of being compelled to fight in such a war, having grown up with the only peacetime draft in American history. After the Korean War, the Universal Military Training Act had had only a limited effect on the lives of the young. Because manpower needs were exceeded by the supply of young men coming of draft age, students and young married men generally were able to avoid military service. The escalation of the war after 1964, however, by increasing the number called into service, made the draft a threatening presence in student life. Now, a generation that had been raised to a high sense of destiny was confronted with the prospect of becoming cannon fodder in a dubious foreign war. As monthly draft calls rose from 10,000 to 30,000, Selective Service began to limit student deferments to those who remained in good academic standing or scored high on a special aptitude test.

Most students acquiesced to the draft, some embracing it as a matter of patriotic duty, though more than a few others found loopholes to escape service in Vietnam. In 1966 alone, some 650,000 took draft deferment tests. Nearly half a million chose to study for such exempt professions as the ministry, teaching, and engineering, and still others were part of the more than 1 million men whose service was safely limited to the National Guard or the reserves. There were those, however, who refused any military service. Some of these sought exemption as conscientious objectors; some declined to register for the draft; and some—perhaps as many as 20,000—fled to Canada.

In their resistance to the draft, the young had the support of Dr. Benjamin Spock, who had often influenced the way they were raised as children. The man known as the nation's baby doctor, concluding early that the war was "militarily hopeless, morally wrong, and politically self-defeating," toured the country—often at his own expense—to condemn it.[4] Like many of the young, he believed that he had been betrayed by American leaders whose policies had often brought the nation to the brink of nuclear war. So vigorous was his attack that in 1968 he was tried for conspiring to obstruct the Selective Service system and was sentenced to two years in prison, a punishment eventually annulled.

Most student radicals chose to challenge the draft and the war head-on, even those who had a good chance of qualifying for a deferment (various studies indicated that activists tended to be better-than-average students). Especially in the beginning, they protested the inequality of the Selective Service process, contrasting their own favored status with the far greater risks facing disadvantaged youth. As their own risks began to increase, however, they took a stand on more personal grounds, generally by objecting to forced conscription into a war that they considered odious and immoral. "We are not afraid to risk our lives," said Paul Booth of SDS. "We have been risking our lives in Mississippi and Alabama, and some of us died there. But we will not bomb the people, the women and children of another country." In April 1965, some 15,000 people participated in an SDS-organized rally in Washington, DC, where they heard Paul Potter, SDS president, first call for a "democratic and humane order" for all people and then condemn "the incredible war in Vietnam" as having destroyed the illusion that morality and democracy were the guiding principles of American foreign policy.[5]

In October 1965, *Senior Scholastic*, the national weekly for high school students, reported that increasing numbers of students were opposing the draft on the grounds that it was "incompatible with democracy and unsettling to youth."[6] Convinced that political demonstrations were not enough, SDS leaders launched more direct attacks on the draft machinery, both by urging public opposition to it as undemocratic in its arbitrary choice of who was to be sent off to die, and by encouraging personal refusals to be drafted. They hoped to extend this effort throughout high schools as well as colleges, intending especially to reach into lower-class neighborhoods where the chances of conscription were greatest. Actually, SDS had little effect in such neighborhoods, in part because lower-class youth were less inclined to question authority. It did, however, encourage some antiwar protesters to dramatize their opposition by turning in or burning their draft cards. In reference to the extensive use of napalm in the war, it urged students to "burn draft cards, but not children."[7]

A great part of the student effort was made in their own universities, which they tried to dissociate from the national war machine—not an easy assignment, since research-oriented university departments often had extensive contracts with the military. In March 1965, students and faculty at the University of Michigan held the nation's first "teach-in," attended by some 3,000 who met to discuss the war and decide what to do about it. Its basic purpose was to challenge the official version of the aims and character of the conflict. The high point was a midnight lecture by Professor Kenneth Boulding, who, applying the standards of democracy, declared that the "the poorest peasant in Vietnam should have as much right as the richest American."[8] This event was soon followed by the more massive "Vietnam Day" at Berkeley, where as many as 20,000 students from the San Francisco Bay area met in a thirty-six-hour marathon teach-in. By May the new movement had spread to some thirty campuses. At the University of Oregon, students heard Senator Wayne Morse, one of the earliest opponents of the war, warn all too prophetically that unless existing policy was reversed, "there will be hundreds of thousands of American boys fighting in Southeast Asia—and tens of thousands will be coming home in coffins."[9] Morse was one of a growing number of older

Americans who, like Dr. Spock and Professor Boulding, spoke out in support of student opposition to the war.

Resistance continued to spread. In May 1966, students at the University of Chicago held a two-day sit-in in an unsuccessful attempt to pressure the university into refusing to supply draft boards with class rankings for deferment purposes; such a process, they declared, pitted them one against the other in a competition where the losers faced possible death. The idea sparked more than a score of sympathy protests throughout the country. In the fall, SDS was able to organize student efforts at various universities aimed at preventing those institutions from sending student grades to Selective Service offices.

First at Berkeley and then elsewhere, antiwar students also tried to obstruct armed forces recruiting on campuses, an effort to expel the military from student life, including ROTC programs. ROTC, a principal source of officers for the army, experienced a decline in enrollments from 155,000 in 1959 to 151,000 in 1968, despite the great increase in the student population. By 1967 these efforts to demilitarize the universities included mass protests against recruiters for the Dow Chemical Company, the makers of the jellied gasoline called napalm, which protesters believed had been dropped recklessly on innocent civilians. At the University of Wisconsin the anti-Dow protest, broken up by the local police, resulted in some fifty student injuries, which provoked a massive student protest against police brutality.

Students sometimes took their protests off the campuses and into the streets. In 1965, antiwar protesters from Bay area universities in California attempted to block the movement of troops to Vietnam from the Oakland Army Terminal but were turned back by the police. Two years later a larger force of students and older protesters attempted to close down the Oakland Armed Forces Induction Center, this time to be literally beaten back by the police after heavy fighting in the streets. Seven alleged leaders, most of whom had been involved with SNCC, SDS, or FSM, were indicted for trespassing and resisting arrest but were acquitted after a number of the demonstrators—including professional men, ministers, professors, and a seventy-year-old grandfather—gave testimony regarding police violence against them. A similar attempt was made against the White Hall Induction Center in New York City, with similar results. And in October 1967, antiwar leaders were able to organize a demonstration of 100,000 students and others at the great headquarters of the war, the Pentagon in Washington.

That year saw a rapid expansion of antiwar sentiment among college students, at least in the North. Among the Big Ten schools of the Midwest, radical activists were elected student body presidents at Northwestern, Michigan State, the University of Wisconsin, and Indiana University. Antiwar sentiment extended to many smaller colleges, significantly reinforced by the spread of democracy's children from the metropolitan centers where they had been strongest. In the mid-1960s the explosive growth of the college-age population often overburdened colleges and universities in the Northeast, leading students to look for openings elsewhere. At the same time, ambitious state universities such as Michigan State, Kent State in Ohio, and the State University of New York at Buffalo were eager to recruit the best students they could find. As a result, such places attracted an influential minority of progressive-minded students who brought their activism to once sleepy campuses.

Before the end of 1967, antiwar activity had grown into what its adherents labeled "the Movement," the single most powerful force for an end to the conflict. At many places, "the Movement seemed to be what its name suggested, a pervasive force for social change that drew growing strength from an awakening young. Its members found in it an exhilarating sense of purpose and of comradeship, "discussion groups where the purpose was really to learn rather than show off," wrote one young member, "parties where you didn't need a date, small groups that traveled and marched together in demonstrations."[10] The Movement was a godsend for those many serious-minded young people who had no place in the vapid social life of their peers and who were dissatisfied by the enforced passivity of their university classes. Paul Krassner, an old radical, recalled that it was as if "all the people who had been the only Martians on the block found there had been a Martian invasion."[11]

The time of good feelings, however, soon gave way to increasing hostility and bitterness. "By late '67," recalled the veteran marcher Nora Sayre, "the demonstrations began to resemble boils breaking out all over our body. Wildness replaced the serene as celebratory styles: the word was 'force' not yet 'violence.' "[12] Before long, though, violence became both the word and the deed. During the Pentagon protest, for instance, there were 679 arrests, many of them resulting from the readiness of some demonstrators to fight back against police and soldiers, in marked contrast to the nonviolence of earlier demonstrations. External violence was paralleled by internal conflict within the Movement, which began to come apart. As a result, the years 1967 and 1968 marked a critical turning point in the history of the forties generation: many abandoned their earlier hopes for American democracy and their own ability to effect needed changes in society and government.

What had gone wrong? Part of the answer probably lay in the rapid growth of the protest organizations caused by the escalation of the war. Many of the newcomers seem to have lacked a strong commitment to the spirit of the Movement, the younger ones having been less exposed to the influences of the democratic family, progressive liberalism, and the civil rights struggle. The newcomers, recalled SDS veteran Todd Gitlin, often came from conservative households, their activism involving a deep personal and emotional rebellion against all authority, beginning with their parents. Some observers concluded that the growing use of drugs was a major factor. The early members of the New Left were generally informed and thoughtful young people who had matured before drugs became a youth fashion, whereas their younger counterparts often grew up with at least soft drugs. (One survey of over 400 protesters in 1968 indicated that nearly four-fifths of them used marijuana once a week or more.)

The chief cause, however, lay outside the Movement in circumstances that bulked particularly large in the limited experience of the younger members. If desperation replaced hope, it was because antiwar protests seemed by 1967 to have had little effect in persuading those in authority to slow the bloody pace of the Vietnam War. The prospect of being forced to serve and die in a useless conflict grew steadily for all the young. If violence began to supersede nonviolence, it was because protests had encountered the violence of law enforcement. "Why," asked the black radical Julius Lester (born in 1939), "do we debate, argue and equivocate about using violence when our lives are threatened?"[13] By the end of 1967 a pattern of deep resentment had developed between largely middle-class and intellectually inclined students and generally working-class and physically inclined local police. From the point of view of the police, the protesters were privileged outsiders irresponsibly attacking the local social order, while student activists saw the police as brutal "pigs" whose chief weapon was not the discussion and argument of the democratic family but the bloody nightstick.

Moreover, hopes for raising a mass protest against the war were disappointed by the conservatism and sheer inertia of the population generally, including many of the young. In 1968, for instance, California overwhelmingly elected the conservative Ronald Reagan as governor, supporting a man who had made a career out of attacking young radicals. After three years of effort the student antiwar movement continued to be a minority movement, its strength confined to relatively few campuses. In

1969 a survey of 859 colleges indicated that for the previous academic year nearly two-thirds had experienced no war protests and three-quarters no draft protests; only 2 percent of these institutions reported protests involving 10 percent or more of their students. The future did soon bring a major shift in public opinion against the war, but it was not soon enough for the impatient young, many of whom shared the doubts of one student when he asked, "What has happened to our much-touted morality, our national ideals, and our religious commitments?"[14]

Further, the growing sense of frustration and alienation was fed by profound disillusion with the Democratic Party, which had stood closer than Republicans to student ideals of democracy. As prominent liberal Democrats such as President Johnson and Vice President Hubert Humphrey clung stubbornly to an increasingly bloody and threatening policy, the radical young came to condemn them and "the liberal establishment" for betraying world peace, racial justice, and individual freedom. Where before they had seen liberalism as an ideal incompletely fulfilled, they now condemned its advocates as having failed the cause of peace and justice. Liberals might share the same ideals as radicals, said one activist, but they were "too intimidated by the system to be taken seriously." Another radical went so far as to declare that influential liberals were the "enemy" to be "destroyed."[15] Although this reaction involved only a small minority of the young, it was to have a strong effect in undermining the liberal confidence in government for generations to come.

All these developments left the Movement doubly dependent on another group drifting toward desperation and violence: young African Americans who had grown impatient with the established civil rights leadership. In the early 1960s, civil rights workers had been able to say, in the words of a popular song, "blacks and whites together, we shall overcome." White activists had been heavily dependent on the fight against discrimination for inspiration and direction. SNCC and SDS had been close allies in what was then a nonviolent struggle. By the mid-1960s, however, SNCC was moving away from nonviolence and interracial cooperation toward a militantly racial view of public issues. Early in 1966, for instance, soon after a civil rights worker was shot and killed in Alabama when he tried to use a whites-only restroom, SNCC issued a statement declaring that "the murder of Samuel Younge in Tuskegee, Alabama, is no different from the murder of people in Vietnam" and complaining "that 16 percent of the draftees from this country are Negro, called to stifle the liberation of Vietnam, to preserve a 'democracy' which does not exist for them at home."[16] Under the influence of this new militancy, the relationship between SNCC and SDS shifted from mutual support to a rivalry in which each tended to spur the other toward increasingly radical stands on both the war and racism.

SNCC's changing character reflected changes in America's black population resulting in part from the baby boom. By 1967, over half the black people in America were under twenty-one, a massive new generation whose attitudes had been shaped less by segregation and the old racist system than by the civil rights movement and the expectations it raised. Its members were inclined to measure the distance yet to be traveled to freedom rather than the distance already covered, and they found much reason for discontent. The abolition of discrimination by law was a basic triumph for American democracy, but it did little to improve the condition of the black poor; in fact, although the years of civil rights victories brought considerable economic progress for middle-class African Americans, they also saw a relative worsening of life for the poor, who seemed on their way to becoming a permanent underclass. College-educated blacks suddenly were in demand, but the numerous dropouts from ghetto high schools faced a dim future.

For SNCC leaders and other young blacks, this situation demanded a radically new set of tactics to organize the African American population into a power bloc strong enough to make its needs felt. Looking to the example of such ethnic groups as the Irish, who had created such blocs in the past, the new "Black Power" leaders envisioned a time when strong organization would enable African Americans to achieve an equal place in society on their terms rather than having to accept what the white majority was willing to give them. They believed that doing so required a strong sense of race pride as a basis for confident, united effort.

Eldridge Cleaver, the author of the influential *Soul on Ice* (1968), for instance, warned that blacks would be plagued by divisive self-hatred and feelings of inferiority until they had repudiated the white standard of beauty to which they had been indoctrinated in favor of the confidence that black, too, was beautiful. No longer, as had been true in the past, would their children prefer white dolls to black. Black Power advocates such as Stokely Carmichael, a young SNCC leader, urged the people to develop their own consciousness of themselves and to reject the white man's definition of who they were. It was an idea that many young black Americans were willing to follow in their efforts to escape from the racist past. "There is a growing resentment of the word 'Negro,' " wrote Carmichael, "because this term is the invention of our oppressor. . . . Many black people are now calling themselves African-Americans, Afro-Americans or black people because that is our image of ourselves."[17]

This thinking was natural to a psychology-minded age that empha-sized the importance of self-esteem for healthy human development, espe-cially in the adolescent struggle for self-identity. The new doctrine reflected the growing assertiveness of the black branch of democracy's children. On the other hand, it dealt a severe shock to the civil rights movement; its stress on black self-definition challenged liberal expectations that blacks would simply be integrated into a largely white society. "Integration sim-ply could not be gained," said one advocate of Black Power, "at the ex-pense of black self-worth."[18] And the call for an independent black initiative meant the exclusion of whites from SNCC and other black organizations, no matter how well disposed they were, on the grounds that their pres-ence tended to reinforce the myth of white superiority and the all too frequent reality of black dependency.

In itself, the new black radicalism was no more threatening than the radicalism of the early New Left, but it was born in a time of conflict, a time not simply of the war in Vietnam but also of a series of ghetto riots that intensified the new aggressiveness of young blacks. Of course, the urban ghettos did not embrace the whole of the black experience in America; in the South, black youth continued to be mobilized by Martin Luther King and others in a generally nonviolent movement for change. By the mid-1960s, however, the great migration from the rural South to the cities was a powerful social fact, and in the cities, where the large black population born in the 1940s was reaching maturity in uncomfort-able ways, riots were waiting to happen. James B. Conant warned that the growing mass of jobless and undereducated urban black youth was "social dynamite" that threatened to explode unless their situation was resolved. By 1965, the reporter and historian Theodore White noted omi-nously that because of the high birthrate among urban blacks, the ghettos were experiencing "one of the great population explosions of all time."[19]

The social dynamite continued to accumulate. After 1965, ghetto youth faced the prospect of being drafted into a war in which blacks were suf-fering a disproportionate number of combat deaths and injuries. Although this fact resulted largely from their willingness to risk hazardous duty in order to achieve higher military rank, it seemed to support the charges of black extremists that the war was a racist scheme to exterminate "the cream of young black people" in the interests of white imperialism.[20] On the other hand, the military as a source of employment for young blacks was closed to many by a high rate of rejection for physical or educational reasons. This complicated the problem in ghetto areas, where one or more of every six males ages sixteen to twenty-four was unemployed, and many of the rest held poorly paid jobs with no future.

All too many had limited futures of any sort, since the rate of violent death among young blacks was at least twelve times the rate among whites, chiefly because they were quick to be violent against each other. For people of all ages, the ghetto was a dismal world of high rents for bad housing and high prices for inferior merchandise in ghetto stores. It was a world that seemed rigged against the black poor in favor of outside landlords and merchants. And it was a world subject to the arbitrary will of an outside army of occupation, the police, who were particularly harsh in their handling of unemployed young males, the ones most likely to be on the streets and presumed most likely to commit crimes. Such a challenge to the manhood of ghetto youth generated much resentment against the police.

New York's Harlem was a minefield of such explosive resentments. In May 1964, it was rumored that some Harlem youth had formed a gang called the Black Brothers supposedly to "maim and kill" whites; it was alleged that the gang had already committed four murders. Less than a week later, the President's Committee on Juvenile Delinquency announced that it was preparing a "last hope" program of improved education and job training to "defuse the social dynamite" of Harlem.[21] In the summer of 1964, however, that dynamite exploded following the death of a black teenager at the hands of an off-duty policeman; in the riot that followed, one person was killed and hundreds injured, while dozens of stores were looted.

Harlem set a pattern that was to be repeated often over the next few years. From 1964 to the end of 1968, at least 329 serious riots in 257 cities produced a total of 52,629 arrests, 8,371 injuries, and 220 deaths. In Los Angeles, Chicago, Detroit, and Newark especially, the riots threatened to become open wars between law enforcement agencies and substantial bands of black men, the majority of them from eighteen to twenty-five years old. In July 1967, for instance, years of frustration in Newark's black ghetto burst into violence after the arrest and rumored beating of a black cab driver by the police. Before it was over, at least twenty-four blacks had been killed, including a young man who was soon to be inducted into the armed services.

Tom Hayden, then in Newark as an SDS community organizer, said that much of the rioting was led by "young people with nothing to do and nothing to lose," but that the young had the support of their elders. When the looting began, the young again were in the lead, "breaking windows whenever the chance appeared, chanting 'Black Power,' " concentrating their attacks on white-owned stores and avoiding those owned by their black "soul brothers." As Hayden described the situation, the police and national guard responded like an occupying army, moved by open racism toward acts of "terror" against the people, displaying a trigger-happy disposition in their use of force toward blacks, and systematically breaking the windows of the soul-brother stores that had escaped the looting. Hayden wondered whether the ghettos were not ripe for the development of some kind of long-term guerrilla warfare against the law enforcement authorities: at a time of great distrust of white-controlled institutions, "the role of organized violence is now being carefully considered."[22]

Little actually occurred along this line, but the idea found a much publicized form in the Black Panther Party, founded in 1966 by Bobby Seale and Huey Newton, then young administrators in the Oakland, California, poverty program. Although the Panthers remained young and few, they had a real genius for implanting in the public imagination a picture of themselves as men of militant force. That image was summed up in an issue of *Ramparts* in 1967, which pictured twenty-five-year-old Huey Newton, "Minister of Defense of the Black Panther Party," dressed to the teeth for combat; below the picture was his warning: "The racist dog policemen must withdraw from our communities, cease their wanton murder and brutality and torture of black people, or face the wrath of the armed people."[23] Even though the Panthers had a program for improvement of life in the ghettos, their constructive side was obscured by the glare of their image, which served the fantasies of many bruised male egos but at a heavy cost. Their challenge to the police as racist pigs brought down on them the wrath of law enforcement, and within a few years their leaders were in jail, in exile, or dead.

For a time, however, their bravado did become a powerful force in the increasingly explosive dissatisfaction that had developed in universities as well as in ghettos by the late sixties, a time when the largely middle-class black student population on the nation's campuses had begun to awaken to the new black militancy. At traditionally black and middle-class Howard University in Washington, DC, for instance, a group of students and professors in February 1967 issued a "Black Power Manifesto" calling for the creation of "a militant black university which will counter-act the white-washing black students now receive in 'Negro' and white institutions." As an act of repudiation of the Negro past, the protesters proposed that Howard be renamed Nat Turner University in honor of the leader of the 1831 bloody slave rebellion. After they held a mass demonstration, Howard's president, James Nabrit, dismissed twenty of the student militants and six of their professors. But the Black Power activists remained defiant:

> We gonna lay down our shufflin' shoes
> Down by Nabrit's door
> Ain't gonna shuffle no Goddam more.[24]

This same defiance developed in many of the northern universities where blacks generally had been a small, silent, and ignored minority on campus. During the late 1960s, though, their numbers had grown considerably at some of the major universities, partly because of efforts to recruit disadvantaged blacks. By 1965, well aware of the growing importance of a college education for success, colleges in the Ivy League and elsewhere attempted not only to enroll black students but to make them comfortable with university life. In the New York City area, teams of college admissions officers visited ghetto schools to find likely candidates for admission. Such steps made campuses even more sensitive to the troubled life of the ghetto.

The combination of race consciousness and militancy brought the formation of black student unions and other similar organizations, which tried to create a meaningful place for black minorities in the universities. Color replaced class as the primary consideration, and middle-class students began to adopt the clothes, styles, and language that they believed were authentic to black people. Dismissing most of the established curricula as irrelevant to their needs, the activists demanded the formation of Black Studies programs, to be taught by black professors, in which students could develop race pride and identity as well as acquire knowledge useful to the black community. These demands constituted the leading issue in more than 40 percent of the 221 demonstrations during the late 1960s in the nation's universities—considerably more than those involving the Vietnam War.

One of the most significant of these incidents took place at San Francisco State College. Under the influence of Bay area radicalism, this college, like Berkeley, had long been particularly open to new ideas and practices, including those associated with Black Power. In 1968, African American students began a militant campaign for a Black Studies program that they could control, and they were soon joined by Hispanic American and other minority students who demanded a similar Third

World Studies program for themselves. Before long the two groups, along with the local SDS chapter, held a series of demonstrations that brought them into conflict with the police. Finally, radical leaders called a strike in November 1968, and for a time the campus was closed down amid threats of violence. One black leader urged his followers to bring guns to campus, while SDS reportedly circulated instructions for making bombs, several of which were subsequently exploded on campus. The strike, which also soon involved part of the college staff, became the longest in collegiate history. It was not broken until March 1969 after a series of mass arrests backed by the hard-line administration of Governor Ronald Reagan.

By early 1969, tensions had grown on many campuses. Most universities avoided major conflicts, but violence did erupt at some of the elite institutions where core groups of democracy's children were especially strong. The most dramatic explosion took place on the opposite side of the continent from Berkeley and San Francisco State, at Columbia University in New York City. Throughout most of the decade, Columbia had been one of the more conservative of the major universities, but its very conservatism made the explosion there more powerful. Even more than Berkeley under Clark Kerr, it was a multiversity with strong ties to the national war machine through its Institute for Defense Analysis. Its president, Grayson Kirk, was more concerned with its business operations than with its students. "He hasn't spoken to anyone under thirty since he was under thirty," quipped the playwright Eric Bentley.[25]

One of Kirk's major concerns was to improve the character of the Morningside Heights area surrounding the university by buying up apartment buildings and then evicting their poor black and Puerto Rican tenants. This attempt to create what critics called an "egghead ghetto" at the expense of the poor set the stage for hostility and suspicion when Columbia announced that it was planning to build a new gymnasium on some thirty acres of land to be taken from Morningside Park, which served the needs of the people of Harlem located below the Heights. Rightly or wrongly, observers began to view the university as an institution which, with the support of the local Establishment, was ruthlessly advancing its interests at the expense of poor and powerless black people. Its "Gym Crow" plan raised the opposition not only of Columbia's small Students' Afro-American Society but also of SDS, which had more influence among students.

Mark Rudd, the twenty-year-old newly elected chairman of the local SDS chapter, had already proved that he was a leader of some daring and imagination in dealing with the military. Earlier, he had arranged a special reception for the head of the New York City draft board, who was to speak at Columbia in defense of Selective Service. After the man had begun his speech, a group of students with a fife and drum and some flags created a racket in the back of the room; as all eyes turned their way, someone stationed in the front row got up and pushed a lemon meringue pie into the speaker's face.

It was in part this sort of thing that led the Kirk administration to ban all indoor demonstrations and to warn that it would "not tolerate efforts to make the university an instrument of opposition to the established order."[26] In turn, this ban became a challenge to SDS, which believed that Kirk had turned the school into an instrument of support for a flawed and arrogant order. One student activist, nineteen-year-old James Kunen, probably spoke for many students when he denied that he wanted some kind of revolution; to the contrary, "we are fighting to recapture a school from business and war and rededicate it to learning and life."[27]

On April 23, 1968, SDS combined with the Students' Afro-American Society to hold a protest rally against both the proposed gymnasium and the Institute for Defense Analysis; after the rally a mass of students moved to the Low Library, where President Kirk's office was located, only to find the doors locked. Frustrated, many of them made their way to the gymnasium site, where they tore down a protective fence before the police intervened and arrested one student. Now, thoroughly aroused, the protesters moved to Hamilton Hall, a classroom building and the administrative center of Columbia College, and began a sit-in in support of their right to demonstrate as well as of their demands regarding the gym and the defense institute. Before long, the white demonstrators turned the hall over to their black partners and moved on, eventually occupying four other campus buildings and bringing the college and other elements of the university to a halt.

The sit-in lasted for nearly a week, during which the 800 or so demonstrators maintained their control over the buildings. They tended to be much like student activists and demonstrators on other campuses: the majority of the white students came from upper-middle-class, largely professional families (a significant number had parents who were high school and college teachers), as did a substantial minority of the black students. As elsewhere, they were majoring predominantly in the humanities and social sciences rather than engineering and other technical fields, their radicalism often expressive of resentment and uncertainty over their own place in the heavily technocratic society surrounding them. They were, in one observer's terms, a "young intelligentsia" who feared that they would be made cogs in the repressive system rather than being allowed to work for self-fulfillment and public enlightenment. In their opposition to the campus version of the system, they experienced the heady feeling of being a company of brothers and sisters, members of the same community, able to manage their own affairs against the world. In at least two of their so-called communes, they put into practice the participatory democracy long advocated by SDS (Tom Hayden had joined them), making all members participants in decision-making.

They could not defy the leviathan for long, however. They were only a small minority of Columbia's 17,000 students, most of whom were either indifferent or hostile to the sit-in. And they faced a university administration whose attitude toward student demands agreed with the statement of one faculty member that "whether students vote 'yes' or 'no' on a given issue means as much to me as if they were to tell me they like strawberries."[28] Unwilling to give in and unable to oust the students from the buildings, the administration hesitated to bring in outside force, in part fearing that an attack on the black students in Hamilton Hall might inflame the inhabitants of nearby Harlem; the riots set off by the assassination of Martin Luther King earlier in the month had demonstrated the explosive potential of the ghetto. Finally, however, the administration asked the New York Police Department to clear the buildings.

On April 30 an army of 1,000 policemen moved onto the campus. Fortunately, they were able to persuade the black students to leave Hamilton Hall peacefully, thereby averting trouble from Harlem. Not so fortunate were the white students in the other buildings when they defied police warnings to evacuate. What followed was, as someone observed, probably the closest thing to class warfare that Columbia was likely ever to see: the generally working-class police against upper-middle-class students. The former were resentful of the way the young had abused their privileged position; the latter, resentful of authority, especially that of the uniformed pigs. By the time the increasingly irritated police had finished ordering, pulling, pushing, prodding, dragging, and beating the not always nonviolent sitters-in, more than 150 people, mostly students, had been injured and 712 had been arrested. One lesson was not enough. Three weeks later, when some 350 students again occupied Hamilton Hall to protest efforts to punish leaders of the April revolt, a new police action produced 177 more arrests and 68 injuries.

Defeat, however, became victory, since the next months brought virtually everything that the students had demanded: The gymnasium was not built in Morningside Park; Columbia eventually severed its ties with the Institute of Defense Analysis; President Kirk's ban on indoor demonstrations was soon lifted, and he himself resigned his position. And for good measure, the university eliminated some of its restrictions on student life. On the other hand, though, the victories helped undercut the movement; as the tensions of 1968 eased, many students fell away from the radical cause. In 1969 the local SDS chapter attempted a new sit-in but found little student support. This new action was dismissed by the Columbia *Daily Guardian*, which had supported the 1968 strike, as "an ugly episode in the corruption of the radical movement," one that promised little good for the future. In place of the free, open, and democratic character of the early SDS, the newspaper noted a narrow sectarianism on the part of the radical leadership, an intolerance of dissent that cut them off from the rest of the campus: "In their weakness and isolation, they turned bitter, divided and violent. They carried clubs as a matter of habit in the buildings."[29]

This bitter spirit was evident in the pronouncements of radical student leaders in the following months. The generally level-headed Tom Hayden proceeded to proclaim approvingly that the students were becoming a revolutionary force: "They want a new and independent university, standing against the mainstream of American society, or they want no university at all. They are, in Fidel Castro's words, 'guerrillas in the field of culture.' "[30] But it was left to Mark Rudd, a leader of the Columbia revolt, to reach the peak of revolutionary rhetoric. In an article published in the *Saturday Evening Post*, Rudd declared that the strike, far from being an internal affair, was directed against the entire politico-economic system of the nation, a capitalist system that had subordinated the university to its racist and imperialist policies. Since the university could not be "free" until society was freed from such domination, students were beginning to see the importance of allying themselves with all the victims of the System, with "black people, . . . Mexican-Americans, . . . the Vietnamese people, and with the exploited and oppressed throughout the world. We intend to unite with all people who believe that men and women should be free to live as they choose, in a society where the government is responsive to the needs of all the people, and not the needs of the few whose enormous wealth gives them the political power. We intend to make a revolution."[31]

That extremism was linked to a dogmatic disposition increasingly common among student radicals. Those like Rudd thought there should be no toleration of those who did not identify with the oppressed and who did not strive to turn the university into a force against oppression:

"Either you support the oppression of human beings or you fight against it."[32] Such dogmatism threatened to politicize higher education in the worst possible way. Whereas the FSM had fought for the right of students to organize for political action off campus, and where students in many places had fought for some greater influence on university policy, Rudd and others demanded a university dedicated to *their* idea of what was right. This arrogant insistence that everyone accept what the radicals believed served only to polarize people in a game of pros and cons in which the conservative opposition had by far the stronger hand. In fact, the Rudds of the student movement served not only to feed a right-wing backlash but also to antagonize many liberal-minded students and others who had supported the efforts to eliminate racism and the war.

The more the extremism of these radicals tended to isolate them even from their friends, the more they tended to drift into apocalyptic fantasies of some great confrontation with the System. In late 1967, for instance, a writer in *The Nation* warned that a growing number of those in the antiwar movement were coming to condone and even to advocate violence under the influence of a "guerrilla mystique," the cult of heroic personal action against faceless power.[33] Inspired by the example of the Black Panthers and of Fidel Castro in Cuba, more than a few young Americans had come to dream of themselves as guerrilla fighters against a ruthless establishment which eventually they would overthrow by force.

Such tendencies had their explanations. There was the ever escalating violence of the war abroad and the violence at home: ghetto riots, the assassinations of John Kennedy, Robert Kennedy, and Martin Luther King, and police attacks on students. There was the deceitfulness of the government and its abuses of power, especially its claim of the right to force the young to fight and die in a foreign land. There was enough to persuade those who wanted to be persuaded that they did face a tyrannical and brutal System. Whatever the explanations, the important point was that a small but vociferous faction of the young had lost faith in American society and in the processes by which society could be improved.

After World War I there had been what was called the Lost Generation of young people dissatisfied with America. Now, in the midst of another war, the nation which for most of its people was the freest, richest, and greatest country in the world was beginning to lose a part of its young to the conviction that it was instead the curse of the world. To democracy's children, it was betraying the ideals that they had learned in the decades before. For radical students the recourse was to dream dreams of violent revolutionary upheaval. For many other young Americans, though, it was to drift off into another world of fantasy which they took to be the world of the future. While the radicals pursued what was becoming an apocalyptic form of politics, other young rebels chose to place their hopes in a new culture fundamentally different from the corrupted culture that seemed to threaten their idea of freedom and happiness. They believed that from cultural rather than political revolution would come the new democratic world in which all would be free—free in ways especially wanted by the young.

NOTES

1. Betty E. Chmaj, "Paranoid Patriotism," *Atlantic Monthly* (November 1962): 91–97.
2. Richard E. Peterson, "The Scope of Organized Student Protest," in Julian Foster and Durwood Long, eds., *Protest: Student Activism in America* (New York, 1970), 76.
3. Butz, *To Make a Difference*, 160; Edward Simpson, "Student Activism," *Journal of Social Issues* 23, no. 3 (1967): 29–30.
4. Robert K. Massie, "Not THE Dr. Spock," *Saturday Evening Post* (May 7, 1966): 61.
5. "Draft Riots on College Campuses," *School and Society* 93 (1965): 420; Miller, *Democracy*, 251.
6. *Senior Scholastic* (October 28, 1965): 6–8; Miller, *Democracy*, 232; Edward J. Bacciocco Jr., *The New Left in America* (Stanford, CA, 1974), 146.
7. Nancy Zaroulis and Gerald Sullivan, *Who Spoke Up? American Protests against the War in Vietnam* (Garden City, NY, 1984), 59.
8. Louis Menashe and Ronald Radosh, eds., *Teach-Ins USA* (New York, 1967), 7–15.
9. Quoted in *New York Times* (May 9, 1965): VI:25, 91.
10. Dick Cluster, *They Should Have Served That Cup of Coffee* (Boston, 1979), 120.
11. Quoted in Ron Chepesuik, *Sixties Radicals, Then and Now* (Jefferson, NC, 1995), 30.
12. Quoted in Nora Sayre, *Sixties Going on Seventies* (New York, 1973), 37.
13. Julius Lester, *Revolutionary Notes* (New York, 1969), 42.
14. Wachsberger, *Voices*, 250.
15. Terry Anderson, *The Movement of the 1960s* (New York, 1995), 201; E. Joseph Shoben Jr. et al., "Radical Student Organizations," in Foster and Long, *Protest*, 218–19.
16. Zaroulis and Sullivan, *Who Spoke Up?*, 79.
17. Stokely Carmichael and Charles V. Hamilton, *Black Power* (New York, 1967), viii, 37.
18. Charles V. Hamilton, "The Black Power Revolution," *Progressive* (February 1969): 29–31.

19. Theodore White, "Why Negroes Riot," *Reader's Digest* (November 1965): 68.

20. Robert W. Mullen, *Blacks and Vietnam* (Washington, DC, 1981), 15, 41.

21. *New York Times* (May 3, 1964): 64; (May 7, 1964): 1.

22. Tom Hayden, *Rebellion in Newark* (New York, 1967), 17, 29–32, 37, 70.

23. Sol Stern, "America's Black Guerillas," *Ramparts* (September 1967): 24–27.

24. Sophie F. McDowell et al., "Howard University," *Public Opinion Quarterly* 34 (1970–71): 383.

25. Quoted in Charles Kaiser, *1968 in America* (New York, 1988), 157.

26. Allen M. Barton, "The Columbia Crisis," *Public Opinion Quarterly* 32 (1968–69): 335–37.

27. James M. Kunen, "Why We're against the Biggies," *Atlantic Monthly* (October 1968): 65–67.

28. Robert Liebert, *Radical and Militant Youth* (New York, 1971), 3–4.

29. Ibid., 243.

30. Tom Hayden, "Two, Three, Many Columbias," in Robert G. Noreen and Walter Graffin, eds., *Perspectives for the Seventies* (New York, 1971), 38.

31. Mark Rudd, "We Want Revolution," in ibid., 42–43.

32. Liebert, *Radical and Militant Youth*, 242–43.

33. Lawrence Grayman Jr., "The Goals of Dissent," *The Nation* (December 11, 1967), 618.

CHAPTER **Eight**

COUNTERCULTURE

A T THE OPENING OF THE NEW YEAR 1967, *TIME* GAVE ITS "MAN of the Year" designation to all Americans who were twenty-five years of age or younger, a selection determined by the fact that young people had come to constitute one-half of the nation's population. Without making any attempt to distinguish among this great mass of individuals, the magazine tagged the young population the Now Generation, which in various ways wanted what it wanted "now" rather than at some future time; there was no tomorrow for these young people, only the immediate moment to be experienced. Although they were, in this view, pleasure seeking, they supposedly practiced an honest hedonism without adult hypocrisy, one especially notable for its absence of sexual inhibitions: "They claim to find the body neither shameful nor titillating." There was, declared *Time*, a deep generation gap between the young and the old, but it promised a better time ahead, since the young had escaped much of the selfish, hagridden past of their parents. This new Man of the Year would "infuse the future with a new sense of morality, a transcendent and contemporary ethic that could infinitely enrich the 'empty society.' " And so the nation's leading news magazine joined the growing number of sycophants of youth, carrying to an extreme the common hope that the new generation would produce moral accomplishments impossible for the old.

The view of the generation gap was not always so positive and hopeful. Conservatives in particular continued the tradition of adult skepticism and concern regarding the apparent waywardness of youth. In the mid-1960s, however, it was the fashion to see the new generation as bearers of a new and better future. A month after the *Time* article, for instance, *Look* magazine chimed in with its own version of the generation gap. In *Look*'s view, the young were the product of a new age of affluence, modernism, nuclear arms, television, the civil rights movement, and other influences that had left them unwilling to accept either the authority or the ways of the parent generation. Affluence especially had persuaded them to reject the old Calvinistic ethic of self-restraint and work in favor of a freer life, one to be enjoyed rather than sacrificed to competition with others for money and power.[1]

These pronouncements had some logic to support them. The new generation had grown up in a postwar world of affluence, Cold War conflict, and nuclear danger distinctly different from the times of their parents. But the generation-gap idea was another glib generalization compounded more from various bits of popular thought than from a close study of reality. Actually, the young in general were far more likely than not to have derived their ideas and their attitudes, radical as well as conservative, from members of the older generation, often from their own parents—as was the case with many of the radical students. Moreover, tradition continued to have a powerful influence over both generations in many sections of the country, especially in the South, the region most resistant not only to changes in racial relations but also to the peace movement and other radical causes. Elsewhere, too, strong ties still existed between the generations, supported by the institutions of traditional education. Conservative religions continued to shape the minds and morals of the young, especially in rural areas, and the schools continued to be strong influences for traditional values. Although the major universities often had substantial numbers of radicals, even in these the generation gap was more apparent than real: one study of three distinct groups (left, right, and conventional) at a major midwestern university revealed that the students in each group—even the radicals—generally shared the values of their parents.

One of the strongest of connections between the generations was organized sports. As never before, athletic contests in football, baseball, basketball, and track on the high school and college levels drew millions of spectators and tens of thousands of participants. The 1960s saw a significant and conspicuous withdrawal of upper-middle-class youth from competitive sports, but many others took their places. For most athletes and their coaches, organized competition among males, like the hunt and like war in the past, provided a field where the participants could prove their manhood. This was especially the case with football, which grew in popularity despite sporadic complaints against it.

The sports culture had a widespread and generally conserving influence, often in unexpected ways. During the sixties, college sports programs began to break from the generally segregated white teams of the past and to recruit able and ambitious black athletes from ghetto areas. Much of this was done via a kind of Underground Railroad manned by local managers of ghetto teams; one such manager who ran a local sports club for underprivileged kids in Detroit had contacts with colleges throughout the nation. The recruitment of often poorly educated ghetto youth brought the bending of college admission and program requirements in ways that disturbed many educators, but it also served some desirable social ends: it both furnished a way out of the ghetto for thousands of underprivileged youth and, in doing so, created a great involvement in sports that kept many of the biggest and strongest of young males out of trouble. The Underground Railroad for black athletes was undoubtedly a major force for the reduction of explosive tensions in ghetto areas.

Competitive athletics were generally an integral part of school culture, furnishing local heroes for much of the student population and also providing opportunities for the nonathletic to participate in sports rituals. Probably, the greatest opportunity was provided by the marching bands—an evolving American art form that accompanied virtually every football team—and the cheerleading squad, the traditional place especially for young women to shine. Generally, the cheerleaders, male and female, were closely aligned with the fraternity-sorority world. And generally they were conservatives, the upholders of traditional values and conventional behavior. The rare exception proved the rule: in 1968, radical Berkeley elected a peace activist as its head cheerleader, but he was booed into quick retirement when he both confused and annoyed the crowds at basketball games by trying to lead them in such peppy yells as "End the war, end the war" and "Ban the bomb."[2]

Organized competitive sports did come under attack among some circles of the forties generation, especially among the advantaged young. A senior at private Andover Academy, for instance, reported in the late 1960s that student intellectuals had replaced athletes as the respected ones there—and that interest in sports had given way to interest in sex and drugs. For every school that dropped sports competition, however, there were probably a hundred that organized their more aggressive and physically able students into competitive teams. The huge and growing addiction of Americans of all ages to watching athletic contests generated powerful support for sports programs. With their emphasis on group competition, conformity, and discipline, such programs did much to prepare the young for roles in what radicals denounced as the System.

Sports often had at least a marginal relationship to one other traditional form of youth activity, the nonpolitical riot. The annual football contests between Texas and Oklahoma in the Cotton Bowl, for instance, were celebrated in downtown Dallas each year by thousands of "adolescent drunks, screaming and shoving and reeling against walls, surging up and down sidewalks and gutters."[3] In 1964 a mob of 700 students celebrated St. Patrick's Day by trashing the Hotel Commodore in New York. The same year saw the arrest for drunkenness and disorder of some 1,400 of the 75,000 students gathered for spring break in Florida at Daytona Beach. And in 1967, vacationing students rampaged in Fort Lauderdale, attacking vehicles and battling with the police. These and other incidents proved that it didn't take opposition to the draft or to the war to evoke youth violence.

The culture accepted by these student rioters and by the majority of American youth tended to be a conservative one, but there was a prominent minority who did in some respect rebel against the dominant culture, often under the inspiration of older critics of existing society. By the mid-1960s, many of the young rebels announced themselves through their appearance. The growing preference of many young men for beards and long hair and of young women for an unpermed, unrouged, and often unkempt look was an obvious rejection of conventional social norms. The efforts to ban the new fashions from the high schools, on the grounds that sloppy styles meant sloppy minds, led to numerous civil liberties protests by rebellious students in the name of the right to be themselves

Along with their looks and their clothes, rebellious youth had their own defiant music, particularly in the new forms of rock music that appeared in the middle and late 1960s. Following the lead of Bob Dylan, the college crowd turned from the simple folk songs of protest in the early part of the decade to increasingly complex blends of folk and rock, whose sounds and lyrics often did seem intended to offend and repudiate adult conventions. "Consider how small you are," the popular Jefferson Airplane group told the public. "The human dream does not mean shit to a tree."[4] And its well-known associations with drugs and sex seemed to make rock music a culturally revolutionary form, condemned as such by many and also acclaimed as such by many others.

Although its overall control generally was in the hands of adult entrepreneurs interested in making money rather than promoting a revolution, the new music, along with the beards and long hair, seemed to indicate that the forties generation was becoming a powerful force for radical change in American culture and, by extension, in American society as a whole. If hopes for political revolution seemed destined to frustration and bitterness, there was always the prospect for a powerful cultural revolution that would forever alter the way Americans thought and felt about life and, by so doing, fundamentally change their behavior toward the world and each other. Youth was "a truly unique force for which there is no precedent," wrote one of the hopefuls, "an essentially nonpolitical force, a cultural force, that signals, while it can't by itself initiate, the probable beginning of a new millennium."[5] There was much talk about the emergence of a "counterculture" which, if only guided right, would introduce a better age.

The idea of a counterculture, like many of the other powerful ideas of the 1960s, had its origins in previous decades. In this case, it was the thought and example of the "beatniks" or "Beat Generation," who had appeared after World War II. The Beats renounced the "rat race" of everyday living in the hope of attaining some personal religious experience to unlock the potential for creativity, love, and joy that they believed existed in each of them. With the help of drugs and uninhibited sex, they sought a heightened awareness both of their own inner selves and of some transcendent existence beyond the mundane world around them.

The Beat style had little influence on the overwhelming majority of the young, but its openly contemptuous rejection of contemporary society had attracted more than a few discontented youth in the high schools and colleges by the late 1950s. Seeking at least temporary escape from what they felt was suffocating conventionalism, a new generation of would-be cultural rebels flocked to the coffeehouses that had sprung up in the larger cities, to listen to Beat poetry and music amid the promised sweet life of an exotic world. Although few were ready to accept the outcast status of the original Beat rebels, the mounting outrage of parents and teachers over "beatnik" beards, jeans, manners, and slang indicates that the Beat world had become an influence on the forties generation. By the early 1960s, many of the young had read Jack Kerouac's classic, *On the Road*, and the published poetry of Allen Ginsberg and Lawrence Ferlinghetti. Although conservatives were prone to see the beatnik as an irresponsible bum, the influential novelist Norman Mailer proclaimed him "the torch-bearer of those all-but-lost values of freedom, self-expression and equality."[6]

By the mid-sixties the Beat attitude had been absorbed by enough young rebels to raise hopes that a major transformation of American culture and society was under way. These hopes were formalized by, among others, Theodore Roszak in *The Making of a Counterculture*, a book significantly subtitled "Reflections on the Technocratic Society and Its Youthful Opposition." Like numerous other intellectuals, Roszak had little use for modern society, which had "given us a proficiency of technical means that now oscillates absurdly between the production of frivolous abundance and the production of genocidal munitions." He warned that Americans confronted a subtly totalitarian society that dominated the thought of those who belonged to it, providing an overabundance of material things while limiting and impairing the human potential. Fortunately for humanity, this society was generating the force for its own destruction in the form of a young generation whose upbringing and experiences in an age of affluence had alienated them from technocracy and instilled in them "the saving vision our endangered civilization required." They brought a new consciousness that would eventually subvert the technocratic order in favor of a freer and more humane society.[7]

Roszak's book was one among varied expressions of a psychological radicalism which had risen in an intensely psychological age to replace the economic determinism of the Old Left. Material abundance having disappointed Marxist predictions for the uprising of the working class against capitalism, the new radicals looked to a kind of psychological determinism to prepare the young for the same task. The power for revolution against the existing order was to be found in the new consciousness that seemed to be strongest among those nearest the center of that order, the children of the middle and upper-middle classes. In cultural revolution, in the "postmodern" values and attitudes supposedly gaining dominance over the new generation, could be found the materials for a fundamentally new and better age.

If nothing else, this psychological radicalism gave encouragement to various would-be prophets who tried to educate the young to their version of new consciousness and its results. In *Love's Body* (1966), for instance, Norman O. Brown offered the hope that the expected overthrow of sexual repressiveness would work a revolutionary transformation in the human body, creating a new and exhilarating relationship of people with themselves and with nature. The hazy eschatology of his book was especially evident in its closing lines: "The antimony between mind and body, word and deed, speech and silence, overcome. Everything is only metaphor, there is only poetry."[8]

The same hope for fundamental change in human nature was offered in a distinctly different way by Marshall McLuhan, the Canadian communications expert, who placed his hopes in the influence of television on the young. In his *Understanding Media* (1964) and other works, McLuhan ("the medium is the message") excited much controversy by arguing that steady television-watching was—happily—eroding the old habits of thought derived from centuries of preoccupation with the printed word. The decline of literacy which had begun to worry some critics was for him an exciting step toward a better form of human existence, because the new electronic medium was conditioning the young to form intimate "tribal" relationships, restoring the sense of community on a global basis and ending the profound alienation that had haunted modern man. At least two surveys of student reading in 1966 seemed both to confirm and to deny McLuhan's importance in disclosing that although roughly one-quarter of the students had heard of him, less than 3 percent had actually read his writings.

These new forms of romanticism were relatively harmless, since they simply presented in unique ways some accepted elements of society. The same could not be said for another prophet, who placed his hopes on a development that society was attempting to stamp out: the growing use of drugs. In 1960, Timothy Leary, a Harvard psychologist, had been turned on by an experience with hallucinogenic mushrooms to the possible use of drugs as a means to alter human consciousness. By 1963, Leary's interest had come to focus on one of the most potent of the growing number of drugs produced by modern chemistry, lysergic acid diethylamide (LSD), already a subject of experimentation by, among others, the Central Intelligence Agency (CIA). Forming the League for Spiritual Discovery (also LSD), Leary launched a quasi-religious crusade to convert the young to drug usage, urging them to "turn on" to drugs, to "tune in" on their inner selves, and to "drop out" of society's rat race. He believed that under conditions prescribed by him, the mass use of mind-altering psychedelics such as LSD could affect a general transformation of human consciousness which would ultimately change all of society in the interests of human freedom and harmony: "The cause of social conflict is neurological. The cure is biochemical."[9]

Although he looked to modern science for the materials, Leary identified his religion with the nonmodern, "ancient underground society of alchemists, artists, mystics, alienated visionaries, dropouts, and the disenchanted young, the sons arising."[10] Leary had some influence over disenchanted youth, but in general he was only slightly more necessary to drug usage than Brown was to sex or McLuhan to television-watching. There were various other psychedelic voices speaking to the young, most notably rock music. Marijuana was apparently an influence on Bob Dylan's popular "Mr. Tambourine Man," which included such lines as "Take me on a trip / Upon your magic swirling ship." The drug trend probably owed less to these voices, however, than to a combination of modern circumstances. One was the steadily growing availability of mind-altering agents such as LSD, and the other was the idleness and discontent of underemployed youth. When combined with peer pressure in a large adolescent population, such factors produced a 322 percent increase in the number of teenage arrests for narcotics violations between 1960 and 1968.

In 1970 the New York State Board of Regents warned that the drug problem had spread to every level of education, from elementary school up, and to every area—urban, suburban, and rural—and to every class and ethnic group in the state. Although acknowledging various causes, the board put special emphasis on the influence of the generation gap, complaining that respect for tradition and parents had given way among the young to a preoccupation with experience for its own sake: "The vacuum in the lives of youth has been filled—pot taking the place of patriotism. The intense drive to divest oneself from dependence on parents and other elders has given way to conformity with the chronological age group. The highest values seem to be the satisfaction of curiosity and the yearning for 'kicks.' Opium has become the religion of the people."[11]

Contrary to such fears, however, drug usage did not permeate the entire youth population; the majority avoided drugs. In 1972 a Gallup poll indicated that only 18 percent of students had tried a hallucinogen at least once, and only 4 percent had done so within the previous thirty days. The percentages were considerably higher among students majoring in the arts and humanities, though, especially at some of the elite institutions with high intellectual standards. Student activists were often at least occasional users, especially in the depressed and frantic late sixties, but studies indicated that the core of the campus drug scene consisted of a different breed. Where activists generally shared their parents' values, committed drug users were likely to be both emotionally disturbed and deeply hostile to their parents and parental values; taking drugs was both an escape from and a rejection of the parental world.

For this reason, there was a close affinity between the student drug scene and an especially significant youth subculture that burst into public view in the mid-1960s, that of the hippies. Although there was no single road to the hippie realm, the most common route ran through the college campus. Its travelers were often middle- and upper-middle-class adolescents who had developed a profound distaste not only for their parents but also for an education that seemed to lead only to their parents' world. In the late 1950s this distaste grew stronger when the schools increasingly emphasized educational excellence both to fight the Cold War and to prepare for college. Undoubtedly, many agreed with one high school student who responded to what he thought was a deadening, over-organized, and authoritarian system of education with what was becoming a popular rallying cry: "Fuck it." More than half the students at this particular school reportedly used drugs.

For these youth, going to college was an escape from parents and their controlling ways, but it was not an escape from parental expectations. Confronted by a new set of demands whose fulfillment only brought them closer to the hated world of their elders, they soon grew dissatisfied with college life. In this, they were encouraged by the discontent of the growing number of student activists, but unlike those who fought to change the university, these dissidents responded by dropping out. In the larger universities they were joined by enough like-minded dropouts to form little enclaves or "hippie ghettos" near the campuses. Here they could enjoy the security of a new version of the adolescent peer group: families without parents, founded on a common hostility to parental lifestyles.

Lacking any particular social philosophy of their own, these young dissenters were guided primarily by the aim of creating lives as opposed to middle-class life as possible. Where the one taught the importance of cleanliness and appropriate dress, the hippies chose rarely to wash and to wear the most eccentric clothes they could find: military uniforms, cowboy vests, bib overalls, and sack dresses; Indian headbands and felt hats; sandals and motorcycle boots, beads and bells. Where the one demanded clarity of speech and of thought, the other devised a jargon partly borrowed from the Beats and hipsters of the fifties and spoke as if from an intellectual fog. Where the one could be accused of an excessive concern with material possessions, the other practiced a voluntary poverty. Where the one gravitated toward the suburbs, the other chose to live in the decayed housing of the inner city. Where the one urged the importance of marriage, the other practiced an extended form of going steady by living together without marriage. Where the one preached, if not practiced, the virtues of sobriety, the other sought to get high through drugs. Where the one demanded preparation to enter the adult world, the other struggled to remain adolescent. And so the hippie life was a rebel life—an anarchism—infused less with social vision than with rage at the world.

Negativism had its virtues. It was a much needed slap at the stuffy face of contemporary propriety and a much warranted condemnation of convenient hypocrisies. Even more, it generated a new opposition to the standing evils of the times—racism, materialism, militarism, and the neglect of the poor—in the interests of peace and love and brotherhood. And the hippie ghettos provided a much needed refuge for young people not ready for the world. There were places to experiment with life and to strive for individual identity free from unwanted pressures, to find one's talents and to pursue one's dreams, to learn to live and to learn to love, to sit and rap at length with one's adopted brothers and sisters amid the drowsy sweet smell of marijuana smoke. It was the troubled adolescent's version of the sweet life, of memorable joys and experience.

For most, however, it was an ephemeral life. Despite their vehement distaste for the conventional world, the hippies depended on it—on the universities for their intellectual and social life and on parents and society for the money they needed even in voluntary poverty. A few found their way to some kind of independence as writers, artists, or craftsmen, but most could not escape their dependence. Eventually, the majority wearied of their shabby fantasy world and returned to the straight life. For others, though, the hippie ghetto was a way station on a longer journey. In part because of the drug trade, a network connected the university ghettos, encouraging the more venturesome to take to the road. The summers saw a mass migration from place to place by means of hitchhiker's thumb, motorcycle, and Volkswagen beetle or bus. The more dedicated and the desperate gravitated toward the centers of hippie life that had appeared in the major cities, where they could find a more developed and seemingly permanent refuge from society.

On the Atlantic coast the wanderers converged on a section of New York City's Lower East Side called the East Village, a reminder of a better bohemia of the past, Greenwich Village. There they found a welcoming social life that in some ways was reminiscent of the pioneer stage of American society. Having rejected many of the agencies of conventional society, the hippies had to create their own. There were hippie stores, a newspaper called the *East Village Other*, and such services as "the Communications Company," which supplied newcomers with information regarding available housing. One eighteen-year-old girl said of the scene that "everybody just loves each other; there's no hate. Everybody shares. It's just like brothers and sisters."[12] During the Newark riots, they banded together to send seven truckloads of food to people in the riot-torn areas, some to be distributed by Tom Hayden's community-organizing group. There were enough sympathetic inhabitants in the area for many to form "tribes" of like-minded people to share housing and to pursue such joint interests as the theater, moviemaking, music, and publishing. Because the area attracted some people with serious interests and talents who were looking for cheap space and a stimulating atmosphere, it became a significant center of avant-garde culture in the sixties.

The East Village, however, was overshadowed by a flashier counterpart that had appeared on the other side of the continent. The Bay area was the mecca of hippiedom in part because of the radical climate of its universities but also because of rock music. By the mid-sixties a combination of heady cultural climate, electric guitars, and extensive use of psychedelic drugs had produced the "San Francisco Sound" associated with such popular rock groups as Jefferson Airplane and the Grateful Dead, which attracted national and international attention. The scene also nurtured the most powerful and soulful of the rock singers in Janis Joplin, a Texas-born misfit who—with the possible exception of Grace Slick of Jefferson Airplane—was the most widely admired female rock star of the times. It was Joplin who perhaps best summed up the hippie outlook in one of her songs:

> If you get it today
> You don't need it tomorrow
> Because tomorrow never comes, man.
> It's all the same fucking day, man.[13]

For a time, San Francisco was the music capital of the world, the focus of more than 150 rock groups in the Bay area.

The area had not only the largest university hippie ghetto, at Berkeley, but the largest hippie center in San Francisco's Haight-Ashbury district, where some 6,000 to 10,000 hippies lived. "Hashbury" or "Psychedelphia," as it was often called, had the most thriving drug culture in America (estimated use of marijuana and stronger drugs among its hippie inhabitants was reported to be 100 percent), complete with its own newspaper, the sporadically issued *San Francisco Oracle*, which was supposedly financed by drug dealers. For a brief time, it looked as if a counterculture had come to life in the form of an independent urban society inhabited by youthful escapees from the madness of the conventional world.

Ideally, it was the world of the "flower child," the holy innocent liberated from the inhibitions of straight society to be his true self, to do her own thing, in harmony with peers and with the natural world. It was a place to work creatively, free from the inhibitions of conventional forms. It was a place to experiment with not only new drugs but new religions—especially those that had been imported into California from Asia—in the search for a new consciousness. It was a place also to experiment with new social forms. "In the Haight-Ashbury during the last year," declared the hippie *Berkeley Barb* in 1967, "there was none of the shut-in paranoid one-man-and-woman-and-children family structure. Most people lived in communes because they were open and fun. People taught other people what they knew, whether it be about guitar playing, printing presses, dope, confronting slumlords, cooking, . . . painting, sex."[14] In a world where like-minded souls supported one another, who needed the institutions of the parental world? It was a grassroots participatory democracy.

The dominant mentality of Hashbury found its most active expression in the Diggers, a group of hippie activists who developed an ethic of communal self-help with a revolutionary flair. Although they were anarchists who believed that everyone should be free to do his own thing, they also preached the virtues of voluntary cooperation: "Collective energy is so much greater than any one person's, and even mediocre people can do more when they're together in a group."[15] Living together in cooperative communes, they spent part of their time feeding their hungry brethren with food they had scrounged from neighboring supermarkets. They ran a Free Store filled with clothes, furniture, and anything else they could find in a throwaway society, all free to those who needed them, and they dreamed of free medical clinics and various other services. The heralds of a post-scarcity society, they believed that it was possible to live free on the abundance produced by modern technology. Regarding the idea of private property as, to use the most overworked word of their culture, "bullshit," they urged people simply to take what they needed for their own use.

The Diggers were closely aligned with another significant hippie movement, street theater. Convinced that theatricals could be used as tools to attack social evils, hippie dramatists and actors designed plays intended to excite the involvement of people in various causes. They launched theatrical attacks on their pet enemies: the military, racists, parking meters, the local phone company (they presented ways to avoid paying for phone calls). By 1967 the Digger spirit had spread to New York's East Village, where it mixed with an established tradition of street theater to produce even more provocative results—especially after it converted Abbie Hoffman, a master of provocation, to its tactics. To demonstrate their contempt for money, Hoffman and friends got into the gallery of the New York Stock Exchange and threw down handfuls of dollar bills on the stock traders below. Another group formed the "Motherfuckers," a kind of theatrical street gang against the system. In 1968 the group showed up at an SDS convention to disrupt proceedings, waving the black flag of anarchy.

For a time, the hippies became a favorite of the mass media, leading one critic to grouse they had become a fad like the hula hoop and the twist. In early 1967 the inhabitants of Haight-Ashbury hosted a "Human Be-In" in Golden Gate Park, where more than 10,000 people listened to Timothy Leary, the Beat poet Allen Ginsberg, and others. Observers were impressed by the peacefulness of the crowd. Within months the major magazines began publishing articles on exotic Hashbury. In April, *Look* printed "The Love Hippies," followed a few months later with "Inside the Hippie Revolution," written by a twenty-five-year-old reporter who had grown a beard in order to blend in with the revolutionaries. Jack Newfield, the liberal columnist, complained that the attention given to the hippies was at the expense of worthier causes: "Because they are not a real threat to anything they are used to goose a lifeless middle-class, and are even widely imitated."[16] Nevertheless, some magazines took them seriously as a possible harbinger of the future. In its article "The Flower Children," *Time* called them "a growing phenomenon that has not yet reached its peak"; an author in *Trans-Action*, a popular sociological journal, declared them the pioneers of a radically new society in explanation of his title, "Why All of Us May Be Hippies Someday."[17]

What was usually overlooked in all this attention was the fact that the hippies, out of a youth population of many millions, numbered no more than a few hundred thousand generally troubled young people shaken by troubled times. And even as the articles were being published, the centers of the movement were experiencing difficulties of their own. Both Haight-Ashbury and the East Village were attempts by troubled middle-class youth to carve out an existence for themselves in urban slum areas, whose poor inhabitants resented their affectation of poverty as well as their peculiar manner. As a result, rising tensions between the two groups were marked by robberies, beatings, rapes, and murders of the invaders. The tensions were increased by the publicity given the hippies, which attracted thousands of disaffected teenagers, many of them runaways, as well as a variety of psychotics and hustlers. As the populations of Hashbury and the East Village ballooned, so did the problems caused by overcrowding and loose living. Cases of venereal disease skyrocketed, as did those of hepatitis, tuberculosis, and food poisoning. And with them came growing troubles resulting from the abuse of drugs, leading one hippie to revise Timothy Leary's rallying cry to "Tune in, turn on, drop dead."[18]

Soon, many of the more committed hippies began to leave town, fleeing to a new frontier far beyond the cities, to places where land was cheap and people were few. There they set up rural communes, trying to realize the dreams of freedom and brotherhood conceived in city slums in what they hoped would be a paradise of nature. Some of the first were "open land communes," communities of perfect anarchy without rules or expectations, where everyone was free to settle on the land as he or she pleased. Many others had a more collective form and more definite goals. Such was the case of the Hog Farm, an urban commune that transplanted itself to a few borrowed acres previously used for raising hogs. Unwilling and unable to depend on farming, the Hog Farmers became adept at the hippie art of creative scrounging, deriving much of the food they ate from supermarket throwaways. But they also gave themselves a worthy mission in life. Acquiring a used school bus, they used it to transport themselves to various hippie gatherings, where they operated as a service agency, providing drinks and food, first aid, crowd control, and entertainment.

The new frontiersmen were ill equipped to cope with the voluntary primitivism they had chosen, a life that lacked the electricity, plumbing, and other necessities available even in urban slums. In 1968, however, they found a survival manual in the *Whole Earth Catalogue*, a compendium of practical and folk remedies for the problems of independent living; by the next year, it had sold some 200,000 copies. The troubled years of the late sixties brought such a proliferation of communes—by some estimates they numbered in the thousands—that a new phase of hippie life seemed to be opening. In 1968 a committee of cultural radicals, including Timothy Leary and Allen Ginsberg, drafted "The Declaration of Cultural Evolution," modeled on the Declaration of Independence, in anticipation of a new society and a new age.

In 1969 the new age had a grand celebration in the three-day Woodstock Music and Art Fair held on a farm in New York's Catskill Mountains. It drew some 400,000 young people who listened to top rock bands and singers and "grooved" with each other, free to love and to get "stoned."

The Hog Farmers, who had been flown in from New Mexico and brought to the site in psychedelically painted buses, provided food, gave medical assistance, and calmed troublemakers with "cool, low-key hippie talk about making love, not war."[19] Seemingly, never had so many people met in such peace and joy.

The Woodstock success excited extravagant hopes for the creation of a hippie nation. "The way I figure it," wrote one enthusiast, "the next pop festival should be a million people and last for a week, the next should be 8 million and last for a whole summer and the next should be everyone on the whole planet and last forever."[20] A few months later, some hippie leaders met at the Hog Farm to consider what to do with the energy manifested at Woodstock and decided to call on everyone who had attended it to contribute a dollar toward the purchase of 400,000 acres of land. The idea was to create an Earth People's Park where land would be free to anyone who wanted to settle on it. Although political radicals viewed Woodstock as a distraction from the serious business of overthrowing the Establishment, even Tom Hayden was swept up in the enthusiasm. Writing after a ruinous split in SDS, Hayden dreamed of a multiplication of "free territories," like Haight-Ashbury and the communes, forming "a nationwide network with the same oppression, the same language, the same music, the same styles, the same needs and grievances: the very essence of a new society taking root and growing up in the framework of the old."[21]

Dissatisfied with what they saw as the lies of Establishment journalism, the cultural rebels expanded their network of alternative journals and newspapers. The underground papers were run by those who saw themselves as cultural and political guerrillas committed to digging up whatever they could find on those in power, to demonstrate how far the Establishment had betrayed the democratic dream. "All of us—gay and straight, black and white, anarchists and centralists, laid back and revved, violent and pacific," recalled Steve Abbott of the *Columbus (Ohio) Free Press*, "a confusing convergence of the disaffected, disenfranchised, disillusioned, and disestablishmentarians—were vaguely united in the belief that the country operated in direct opposition to its espoused values."[22] By revealing the corruption behind the facade created by conventional newspapers, these journalistic radicals intended to help form the counterculture that would eventually make everyone free.

The hoped-for new age, however, proved as evanescent as the morning mists of summer. Within a few years the majority of the hippie communes, which had sprung up with mushroom speed, had disappeared as quickly.

By 1970, Haight-Ashbury had become a disaster area of decay, depression, and despair, many of the more energetic hippies having abandoned it to alcoholics and drug addicts. In neighboring Berkeley the hippies had rallied to transform an empty lot into a People's Park, only to lose it after a pitched battle with a combined force of state, county, and city police who beat, kicked, and shot 100 or so of the defenders. Finally, to emphasize the change, Woodstock was followed in December 1969 by the disastrous Altamont concert outside San Francisco, where the notorious motorcycle gang Hell's Angels, who had been hired as a security force, began beating into a crowd that had pressed too close to the stage and wound up kicking and knifing a young black man to death. It was an ugly time for peace and love.

The hippies often did represent some of the better attributes of their new generation: its urge to create, its idealism, its willingness to experiment, and its commitment to democratic values. With their psychedelic colorfulness and impudent views of established ways, they gave a vitalizing shock to often dull and stuffy times. Although their rejection of material concerns could be irritatingly self-righteous, it was a much needed reminder that life consisted of more than cars and refrigerators and stocks and bonds. If they fell far short of effecting the much heralded cultural revolution, they did, at least, expand Americans' choices in styles of living. But the hippies also personified some disturbing trends among the young. Besides their influence in promoting the use of drugs, they encouraged an anti-intellectualism that weakened the rational foundation of society, replacing it with a mush of occultism, superstition, and wishful thinking. Their tendency to treat history as the irrelevant memory of a defunct and disreputable past left many of the young with little understanding of their real place in time and space. And in their rejection of the middle-class ethic of sobriety, self-discipline, and work, they encouraged a belief that it was better to take from society than contribute to it.

In 1972 a writer in *Ramparts*, complaining of the tendency of dissidents to support themselves in idleness through welfare and food stamps, said that they had come to see America as "a kind of gigantic and bottomless cookie jar" from which they could take without limit. He was soon answered by a pseudonymous "Bob Cratchet" who commended the hippie effort to avoid work as a desirable way of subverting the existing system; it's notable that "Cratchet" was writing from Soledad Prison in California.[23] It was this attitude that encouraged all too many of the young to try to rip off the system, a tendency developed into an art by Abbie Hoffman, who freely offered advice on how to live "on $0 a day" through such means as shoplifting, welfare fraud, using a penny to make a phone call, and crawling under the doors of pay toilets. Hoffman's sometime associate Jerry Rubin preached the same doctrine more romantically— "while looting, a man to his own self is true"—only to have second thoughts when he was the victim of a burglary: "In advocating stealing as a revolutionary act, I guess I didn't make clear the difference between stealing from General Motors and stealing from me."[24] By the 1980s, Rubin had joined the Wall Street rush to make money.

The hippies also served to weaken a civic and public sense among their admirers. Although much of their disdain for society was warranted, it also encouraged a tendency to drop out from any kind of responsible involvement that might help to correct social problems. Although they generally practiced some form of participatory democracy among them-selves, they withdrew from the larger democratic process. As was some-times noted, however, their withdrawal from politics was in itself a form of politics. Advocates of the counterculture idea argued that the expected alteration in consciousness and values among the young would eventu-ally transform the political agenda and system, but such hopes depended on the willingness of youth to participate in the larger process, and this the hippies were unwilling to do. Instead, they retreated from the arena of power into drugs and fantasies, a tactic that often helped transform suspi-cions of power into paranoia, and contempt for politics into anxious pas-sivity. Such an attitude was partly justified by the behavior of the police and other authorities toward them, but in their hostility to government they struck a blow against liberalism, with its belief that government was a democratic instrument needed to achieve democratic ends. Indeed, since liberals often controlled governments, they became worse than conserva-tives in the eyes of the rebels, who saw them as hypocrites pretending a commitment to democratic values that in fact blocked the way to greater democracy.

As a result, many hippies lapsed into apocalyptic thinking, a tendency to see society and government as monsters and the United States as Amerika the fascist state, destined either to be overthrown in some violent up-heaval or otherwise not to be changed at all. It was this attitude that they brought into their demonstrations against authority, a fight of good against evil in which invariably they became the bloodied ones. With the notable assistance of circumstance, their antipolitical attitude and experience in-fluenced many other youth in the middle and late sixties. It was an unfor-tunate situation and time, since it was during these years that the new generation came of political age.

NOTES

1. *Time* (January 6, 1967): 18–23; John Poppy, "The Generation Gap," *Look* (February 21, 1987): 26–32.
2. Pat Ryan, "Once It Was Only Sis-boom-bah!" *Sports Illustrated* (January 6, 1969): 47.
3. Myron Cope, "Texas Football," *Saturday Evening Post* (September 24, 1966): 83.
4. Ed Lermbacher, "The Crash of Jefferson Airplane," *Ramparts* 8 (January 1970): 14–16.
5. Richard Porrier, "The War against the Young," *Atlantic Monthly* (October 1968): 59.
6. Norman Mailer, *Advertisements of Myself* (New York, 1958), 336.
7. Theodore Roszak, *The Making of a Counterculture* (Garden City, NY, 1969), xii–xiv, 1–4, 22–32, 51.
8. Norman O. Brown, *Love's Body* (New York, 1966), 266.
9. Timothy Leary, "In the Beginning," *Esquire* (July 1968): 116–17; Timothy Leary and Richard Alpert, "The Politics of Consciousness Expanding," in George Andrew and Sion Vinkenoog, eds., *The Book of Grass* (New York, 1967) 208–10; Sayre, *Sixties*, 265–66.
10. Quoted in Wesley C. Westerman, *The Drug Epidemic* (New York, 1970), vii–ix.
11. Richard Todd, "Alternatives," *Atlantic Monthly* (November 1970): 112–14; *New York Times* (April 12, 1970): 67.
12. "The Hippies," *Time* (New York, 1967): 82.
13. Quoted in *Rolling Stone* (June 8, 1972): 64.
14. Jesse Kornbluth, ed., *Notes from the New Underground* (New York, 1968), 39–40.
15. Sayre, *Sixties*, 291.
16. Jack Newfield, "One Cheer for the Hippies," *The Nation* (June 26, 1967): 810.
17. "The Hippies," 3.
18. David E. Smith et al., "The Health of Haight-Ashbury," *Trans-Action* (April 1970): 35–37.
19. Andrew Kopkind, "Coming of Age in Aquarius," in Noreen and Graffin, *Perspectives*, 91.
20. Fred Silber, "Woodstock," in Sar A. Libarle and Tom Seligson, eds., *The High School Revolutionaries* (New York, 1970), 122.
21. Tom Hayden, "The Trial," *Ramparts* 9 (July 1970): 54–56.
22. Wachsberger, *Voices*, 1:329.
23. "The Food Stamp Controversy," *Ramparts* (June 1972): 14–15; and "Uncle Bob," *Ramparts* (July 1972): 6–8.
24. Abbie Hoffman, "America on $0 a Day," *Ramparts* (February 1971): 48–55; Jerry Rubin, *Growing [Up] at Thirty-Seven* (New York, 1976), 106–7.

CHAPTER **Nine**

POLITICS

ETWEEN 1964 AND 1972 THE FIRST WAVE OF THE BABY BOOM CAME of political age, presenting a powerful new potential for American politics. By 1972 the 30 million Americans born between 1943 and 1951 had reached at least the age of twenty-one, and the impact of youth was increased by the lowering of the voting age to eighteen through the ratification of the Twenty-sixth Amendment in 1971. The reduction of the voting age had been proposed as early as 1954 by President Eisenhower, and it had won the support of various Americans, including the sociologist Harold W. Bernard, who argued that youth was much needed in the political process: "With the population growing older because of increased longevity the pressure of youth is needed to insure vitality and to encourage innovation to meet the evolving conditions of the present."[1] By the end of the 1960s the nation seemed to suffer from the opposite condition, but by then the Vietnam War had added another rationale: that those who were considered old enough to fight were old enough to vote.

The addition of the 11 million baby boomers born between 1951 and 1954 meant over 40 million youth would be eligible to vote in 1972, more than half the number of actual voters in presidential elections during the period. For those who believed in the generation gap, the entry of this mass into politics promised a basic change in public life. That prospect, however, was based on the dubious idea that the young had beliefs fundamentally different from those of the rest of the population, a romantic notion that ignored the fact that "youth" was not a nation but a stage of development. Moreover, change depended on the willingness of the young to enter into the political process, whereas they likely were in general the most lethargic part of an all too lethargic American electorate.

Actually, the difference between the generations was much less than often assumed. During the wartorn sixties, for instance, the polls did register a significant shift of attitude toward the Cold War among the student population. One survey in 1962, repeated in 1972, revealed the shift in the yes-or-no responses of students to such statements as these: (1) The United States must be willing to run any risk to prevent the spread of communism (72 percent "yes" in 1962; only 23 percent a decade later); (2) Pacifist demonstrations are harmful to the best interests of the nation (44 and then 17 percent); (3) The real enemy today is not communism but war (31 and 67 percent). Another survey revealed an especially sharp shift between 1968 and 1971 in the acceptance of the general goals of war: (1) protecting the national interest (54 percent "yes" in 1968, 30 percent in 1971); (2) containing communism (45 and then 29 percent); preserving our national honor (33 and 18 percent). To the majority of the young, the Cold War seemed a thing of the past.

These shifts, however, were paralleled by similar changes among older Americans. A series of Gallup polls, for instance, indicated that the percentage of Americans ages twenty-one to twenty-nine who classified themselves as "hawks" regarding the Vietnam War declined from 41 in May 1968 to 29 percent in November 1969; for those between thirty and forty-nine (a combination of the so-called Silent Generation and some baby-boom parents), from 44 to 34 percent; and for those fifty or older, from 38 to 29 percent. In the early 1970s a study based on an extensive poll in 1970 of Americans eighteen and older revealed some interesting wrinkles in the generational picture. It indicated that the young as a whole, when compared with the older generations as a whole, were less likely to be highly concerned over the war and more likely to accept existing American policy. College-educated youth, compared with non-college youth, were considerably more likely to be opposed to the war, but so were their college-educated elders.

The 1970 survey presented a somewhat similar picture of attitudes regarding the other fundamental issue of the times, race and civil rights. The young, as expected, were more liberal than older Americans on such matters as the right of black people to live wherever they could afford to live, but college-educated youth were no more liberal than college-educated persons aged thirty to forty-nine; the generational gap here existed between the young and middle-aged on the one hand and those over fifty on the other—a clear reflection of the post–World War II revolution in race relations. These young people were indeed democracy's children, there being substantial agreement within the middle classes where the democratic family ideal had been strongest. Non-college youth, however, were considerably more liberal than older non-college people, and this difference accounted for most of the overall gap between the generations on civil rights issues. The polls did suggest a significantly greater generational difference over life-style issues of special interest to the young, most notably the legalization of marijuana (ages twenty-one to twenty-nine were 26 percent in favor versus 6 percent among those who were fifty or older). Elsewhere, though, the difference was not always significant: 46 percent of young adults supported the legalization of abortion, but so did 38 percent of those ages fifty-plus.

At least one important group of young Americans eluded the polls, the hundreds of thousands of servicemen serving in Vietnam, but there were a few indications of their feelings on the war. In the late 1960s, for instance, John McDermott, an antiwar professor, interviewed four soldiers in the field and found that they loathed the conflict at least as much as he did and expressed no resentment of those who had succeeded in avoiding war service. They condemned open draft resisters, however, for betraying the principle that it was "right to fight for your country," a bedrock belief that McDermott attributed to the authoritarian upbringing characteristic of their working-class background. An army psychiatrist likewise observed that although most soldiers kept their opinions to themselves, those who did express a view were largely opposed to the conflict, and he concluded that the patriotism of the average soldier had led him to suppress his doubts about the war: "There is no room in the American Dream for an unrighteous war."[2]

These suppressed doubts might help explain what by 1971 was becoming an unprecedented collapse of military morale, reflected both in the highest desertion rate (73.5 per 1,000 in 1971) in modern American history and also in the increasing use of drugs, estimated to involve as many as 30 percent of enlisted men. By 1970, moreover, doubt was increasingly becoming outright condemnation among servicemen. Although openly antiwar GIs were still a minority, there were enough to provide some basis for the claim of David Cortright that "a large number of American servicemen will no longer risk their lives in a cause which they do not support." Cortright, himself a soldier active with GIs for Peace, was undoubtedly biased but also at least partly correct when he noted signs of the disintegration of military discipline: "Most GIs these days are into rock and roll, long hair or afros, freaky clothing, beads, guitars and dope."[3]

Various other signs of accelerating decline in morale and patriotism among youth in general included a 1969 poll conducted by Daniel Yankelovich, which revealed that 30 percent of college students wished they lived in a nation other than the United States. Most of the young either continued to acquiesce to the war or retreated into cynical indifference, but many of the more idealistic were driven toward disillusionment not only with government but also with liberalism. This critical disaffiliation from the main stream of reform led some young radicals to concentrate their rage on their liberal elders. In the presidential election of 1964 the young had joined the rest of the nation in rejecting the apparently warlike conservativism of Barry Goldwater in favor of the peace and liberal reform promised by Lyndon Johnson; as late as May 1965 a Gallup poll indicated that three-quarters of the twenty-one to twenty-nine-year-old group approved of Johnson's presidency primarily because of his Great Society programs. But then Johnson revved up the war machine in Vietnam at the expense of the Great Society. By early 1967 his approval rating among the young had fallen to 40 percent, leading Arthur Schlesinger Jr. to warn that "a liberal coalition which cannot enlist the support of the young people of this country is doomed to frustration."[4]

Many of the young turned against Johnson for reasons other than a disappointed liberalism (for one thing, he was not winning the war), but it was that disappointment that shaped the political future. It led disillusioned youth to retreat either into apathy or into radical fantasies of conducting war against what they called the corporate-liberal establishment. Combined with ghetto riots and black militancy, the war in Vietnam—the liberals' war—produced the almost explosive growth of student radicalism in 1967 that ballooned membership in SDS. Confronted with a draft that they saw as opposing their right to life, liberty, and the pursuit of happiness, the radicalized young turned to resisting the agencies of government, threatening a crisis of authority in America.

The majority of democracy's children, however, clung to hopes for change within the system. Even at Berkeley, ten times as many students enrolled in liberal programs to help the poor—such as tutoring in ghetto schools—than in SDS. Throughout the country, young lawyers and law students opened hundreds of volunteer law offices to provide legal advice to the poor; by 1968 they had advised some 2 million people on their rights under law. In August 1967 this disposition to work within the system predominated at the annual convention of the NSA, by far the most representative student organization.

The NSA met that year at the University of Maryland under the shadow of a well-publicized revelation that for years it had been receiving secret CIA subsidies as part of that agency's war against Communist influence over students in foreign lands. Although the NSA had decisively broken this connection the year before, the discovery encouraged SDS to hold a counterconvention on the Maryland campus. And that was not the only challenge to liberalism. Early in the ten-day NSA meeting, Timothy Leary appeared to urge the delegates to drop out of society and "to drop into life" by way of drugs, and black student delegates were able to pressure the majority into an unqualified endorsement of the Black Power movement. On the whole, however, the convention rejected both drugs and extremism for a strong commitment to democracy, voting for increased student power on such campus issues as the regulation of student conduct and the curriculum. Even though the majority were critical of the war, they rejected a resolution calling for a unilateral withdrawal from Vietnam. Instead, the convention set up a committee to organize a political campaign against the reelection of President Johnson in 1968.

Given the NSA's influence on hundreds of college campuses, this decision seemed to open the way for a potent challenge to the war and to the Establishment by democratic means. To direct the campaign, the NSA appointed Sam Brown, an antiwar activist who had narrowly lost the election for its next president. Brown, a twenty-five-year-old Harvard Divinity School student, earlier had given up a deferment from the draft and then had openly refused to fight in the war. The son of a conservative Republican businessman in Council Bluffs, Iowa, he had been chairman of the supervisory board of the NSA when it was revealed that the CIA had been secretly subsidizing the association, a revelation that drove him in disgust to embark on a campus speaking tour to denounce both the CIA and the war. The tour brought him into contact with many like-minded student leaders.

At the convention, Brown predicted that the anti-Johnson campaign would soon discover a viable peace candidate, and by the spring of 1968 the student movement seemed to have found its man in Senator Eugene McCarthy of Minnesota. In part because McCarthy neither acted nor thought like a politician, he had a strong appeal for many young people, especially those attracted to such mainstream organizations as the Peace

Corps and the National Student Government Association—the beardless ones who were willing to "keep clean for Gene" in order to distinguish themselves in the public eye from hippies and radicals. Edward Schwartz, who had defeated Brown for the NSA presidency, described them as "socially concerned undergraduates who have not supported draft-card burnings or anti-recruiter demonstrations but have agonized over the seeming futility of restoring hope in America."[5]

Sam Brown soon became student coordinator of the McCarthy campaign, using his established campus contacts to mobilize thousands of young campaigners to support McCarthy in the New Hampshire primary, the first step toward the Democratic nomination. One observer called Brown's New Hampshire organization "the best field organization ever assembled for a political campaign," one that harnessed the talents and experience of many students who had already been politically active on the local level.[6] The effort was much strengthened when in late January the Vietcong launched their Tet offensive which, though finally beaten back, dealt a severe blow to hopes for military victory in Vietnam. When the results of the New Hampshire primary were announced, it was discovered that McCarthy had come in a very close second to President Johnson. Although part of the vote for McCarthy was actually a vote against Johnson's failures to win a military victory, it did seem that the antiwar young had found a viable candidate.

They soon had two viable candidates, since Johnson's growing unpopularity persuaded Senator Robert F. Kennedy to enter the presidential race. Bobby Kennedy was a shrewd and powerful politician who soon attracted many of the more practical-minded young liberals; one poll indicated that in April he had a commanding lead over both McCarthy and Hubert H. Humphrey among young voters, many of whom were awakening to an interest in politics. Especially after President Johnson announced that he would not run for reelection, the competition between these two critics of the war generated much enthusiasm and hope; it looked as if a new day might dawn for the Democratic Party and for the liberal cause.

It proved to be a false dawn, however, and enthusiasm soon turned to bitterness. In June, while celebrating his victory in the California primary, Kennedy was assassinated. Less than two months before, Martin Luther King had also been killed by an assassin. More violence had come to violent times, and hope again became disillusion. Although McCarthy temporarily benefited politically from the elimination of Kennedy from the race, he proved to be an indifferent campaigner, and it became ever more apparent that the next Democratic nominee would be Johnson's vice president, Hubert Humphrey.

This impending victory of the Establishment gave new energy to radicalism and to radical plans for a confrontation at the Democratic National Convention in Chicago. In December 1967, the National Mobilization—a coalition of antiwar and radical groups—had begun to consider some action at the convention, but its leaders could not agree on what that action should be. Two months later the Mobilization authorized Tom Hayden and his colleague Rennie Davis to organize "an election year offensive." Although they considered holding some kind of counterconvention to dramatize what they considered to be true democracy and liberalism, the planners again were not sure as to the details of the offensive except that it should avoid violence and disruption if possible.

Whatever the planning, it was soon confused by the intrusion of another group eager to have their day in Chicago, the "Yippies." At the beginning of the year the Youth International Party had been formed by Abbie Hoffman, Jerry Rubin, and several others to combine the counterculture of the hippies with political radicalism. The Yippies saw themselves as the party of the generation gap, standing for youth against the adult establishment, as Jerry Rubin made clear in his "Yippie Manifesto":

> The war between THEM and Us could be decided by the
> seventeen year olds.
> We offer: sex, drugs, rebellion, heroism, brotherhood.
> They offer: responsibility, fear, puritanism,
> repression.

Although the Yippies were a runt party, notably short on both numbers and political ideas, they had a genius for adapting the outrageous behavior and rhetoric of street theater to their cause. It was as if *Mad* magazine had entered politics. "Number One on the Yippie program is kill your parents," Rubin told one student group. "Our parents kill us at birth—we've got death-before-life, we've got to be reborn again."[7] Perhaps even Rubin was surprised to find that some people actually took him seriously—among them, unfortunately, were the Chicago authorities. The Yippies, as their contribution to the convention, promised to hold a Festival of Life, with free theater, entertainment, and music plus the chance to get stoned en masse.

Here was the ultimate hippie distraction from serious politics, one amplified by the unfortunate overreaction of the authorities to what was

basically juvenile theatrics. Before the convention began, the Yippies announced their pretended plan of attack: "We will burn Chicago to the
ground! We will fuck on the beaches! We demand the Politics of Ecstacy."[8]
This plus such other threats as the one to drop LSD in Chicago's water
supply added to the mounting anxieties. By the time the convention con-
vened in August, the authorities had assembled a mass force of police and
national guardsmen.

The prospect of a street war discouraged many of the young from
coming to Chicago; instead of the expected hundreds of thousands of
demonstrators, only about 10,000 appeared. But the ingredients for conflict were there. At one extreme, the Yippies continued to thumb their
noses at the Establishment, nominating a pig for president; at the other,
the Chicago police force was armed with guns, tear gas, clubs, and a
working-class rage against the spoiled children of privilege and their mock-
ery of authority. Because city officials had refused to grant permits for
most of the planned demonstrations, the police had a clear field for action. On Sunday evening, just before the convention began, they dragged,
beat, and teargassed the Yippies and their allies out of Lincoln Park; one
of those gassed was Allen Ginsberg. On Monday they arrested Tom Hayden
and, after his release, tailed him until finally he was able to escape in a
mad car chase. Hayden spent most of the rest of his time in Chicago
wearing various disguises to help him evade surveillance.

On Wednesday afternoon an antiwar rally became a melee when, after one demonstrator removed the American flag from a flagpole, the
police charged into the crowd. In the evening a broad spectrum of protesters, disgusted by what they saw as Establishment manipulation of the
nominating process, decided to march on the convention site. Lacking a
permit and any clear plan of action, the demonstrators straggled forward,
only to be stopped by the police massed in front of the Conrad Hilton
Hotel. Within minutes and without warning, the men in blue attacked;
they went berserk, clubbing anyone who moved, demonstrators and pass-
ersby alike. It was payback time for the hippies, the Yippies, and all the
rest of the young who had sneered at authority and had spat on and cursed
the police. Unfortunately, it was the most widely viewed payback in history, since it was televised to much of the country.

After he had watched the police attack from his hotel window, the
veteran political writer Theodore White jotted in his notebook the words
"The Democrats are finished," and so they were.[9] Hubert Humphrey won
the nomination, but he also won the contempt of many of the young, a
sad fate for a man who, as a young liberal in the 1940s, had helped launch

the civil rights revolution. For radicals, the events in Chicago constituted one more demonstration of the corruptness of the system. One high school student, who had witnessed the police attack and condemned it as "oppression of an outright fascist nature," concluded that revolution was the only way of saving the nation from itself: "The federal government and the power structure of this country, the military-industrial complex, has become corrupt to the point where there is no hope of a reform movement."[10]

The Chicago affair drove some Americans leftward but impelled many others in the opposite direction. That more Americans blamed the demonstrators than the police for the riot was a reflection not only of a widespread dislike of the Yippies but also of all those who rejected the American dream. One poll of Americans found that 56 percent approved and only 31 percent disapproved of the way the police had handled the situation in Chicago; even among those between ages twenty and twenty-nine, the police won 47 to 41 percent. Above all, the reaction reflected a spreading anxiety over "law and order," an issue that was forcing its way to the center of popular concern. These were years of growing violence: the violence of student radicals, of political assassins, of ghetto riots, and also of crime; in New York City alone, there were 904 murders in 1968, five times the number of murders in all of England. Although it had many causes, this ugliness often was identified with youth and with liberalism, with permissive upbringing and its presumed result, contempt for authority. In this view, the action of the Chicago police was fair retribution.

These feelings were shared even by many of the young, especially those who believed that their work and patriotism had been ignored in the attention paid to rebellious youth. Some of these forgotten baby boomers favored the Republican candidate, Richard M. Nixon, but others found a hero in third-party candidate Governor George Wallace of Alabama. If there really was such a thing as the counterculture, then Wallace was the counter-counterculture candidate, a tough-minded traditionalist hostile to hippies, antiwar protesters, radical students, and "pointy-headed" intellectuals. He had his greatest strength among southern segregationists, but he also appealed to many others, especially young workers in the North. One survey of a sample of young people ages eighteen to twenty-four found in October 1968 that 25 percent were for Wallace and only 23 percent for Humphrey, the traditional friend of labor. Many of the Wallace youth sided with their parents in protests against attempts to integrate their neighborhoods; when in 1966, for example, Martin Luther

King led an integrationist march in Chicago's Marquette Park neighbor-hood, he was met by a mob of stonethrowing youth. Although only some 15 percent of young adults actually voted for Wallace, it was evident that a powerful undertow of conservatism was developing among many of the young. It meant the loss of many potential liberal supporters in the future.

The presidential election of 1968 was a major setback for the liberal cause. Before the election the Yippies had urged the young to celebrate in the streets rather than to vote: "Come all you rebels, youth spirits, rock minstrels, bomb throwers, bank robbers, peacock freaks, toe worship-pers, poets, street folk, liberated women, professional body-snatchers."[11] Many of the young neither voted nor celebrated. Humphrey lost to Nixon by less than a half-million of the 73 million votes cast in the election—an indication of the importance of those youth who had been alienated from him; if they had supported him, he might have won. But the plain fact was that he polled less than 43 percent of the total vote, the rest going to the two conservative candidates. The liberal era that had begun during the Great Depression and had shaped the outlook of the forties generation was drawing to a close, thanks to the political and social backlash that the radicals and hippies had in great measure brought on by their extrem-ism. In 1968, 50 percent of all classes and ages agreed in one poll that "hippies" were the cause of the nation's troubles.

Nixon's victory, combined with the continuation of the war, tended to excite even more extreme attitudes among the radical minority, including sometimes paranoid but also sometimes justified feelings regarding the oppressive tendencies of the times. When, for instance, Tom Hayden was sentenced to prison on charges of conspiring to incite the Chicago riot, he warned that American democracy had begun to harden "into an inflex-ible fascist core."[12] Through a process of natural selection, the times shook out from the mass of activists a minority who became convinced that they were truly oppressed by the nation, a conviction that deepened their com-mitment to the idea of guerrilla warfare and armed revolution. In the summer of 1969 an issue of *New Left Notes* appeared with a cover fea-turing two armed young guerrilla fighters, one black and one white, with the statement, "War can only be abolished through war."[13]

Although one survey of students in the spring of 1969 indicated that the "revolutionaries" were only a small minority (3 percent of all stu-dents), they numbered in the thousands—generally concentrated in and around a few prominent universities—and had a strong voice in the un-derground press. To collect and disseminate news for themselves, radical journalists formed their own press organizations to challenge the establishment views of the Associated Press and other conservative influences on the news. The Liberation News Service, for instance, was founded in 1967 by two recent college graduates, Marshall Bloom and Ray Mungo, who dreamed of making it a democratic cooperative owned collectively by the underground papers. Although they often differed among themselves, these papers did communicate a common world view: they stood for all the world's oppressed, black Americans and Vietnamese peasants, poor people and workers, radicals and peace protesters, and—with the appearance of sex and gender issues—women and gays. And they stood against the Establishment, especially government and its primary law enforcement agency, "the pigs." Their editors saw themselves as underground guerrillas engaged in a war against those in power. Such revolutionary writings generally stirred up no more than an impotent hatred of the police and of the military, but they did help to inspire many of about 250 bombings and attempted bombings of draft boards, ROTC buildings, and other symbols of the Establishment between September 1969 and May 1970.

These acts of violence seemed to be the fiery tip of a developing youth rebellion. According to one survey, the percentage of college students who identified themselves with the radical left rose from 4 percent in 1968 to 8 percent in 1969 to 11 percent in 1970, and the rebellion seemed to be spreading downward into the high school and even junior high school populations. In a scattering of schools throughout the country, the years 1969 and 1970 saw an eruption of active protests. "It's relevance or revolt," one high school student told a group of anxious school superintendents in 1969, "and when it comes to revolt, you haven't seen anything yet."[14] Moreover, rebellion appeared to be spreading out of the schools and into the streets. Following the example of the Black Panthers, Puerto Rican youth in Chicago and New York formed themselves into the Young Lords, a coalition of juvenile gangs with aspirations to organize all gangs into a political force. Although most gangs were concerned mostly with their own neighborhoods, they responded to the temper of their times by proclaiming themselves a "revolutionary political party fighting for the liberation of all oppressed people." It seemed logical, therefore, for Tom Hayden to believe that the old society was losing control over its young and to conclude that revolution was coming: "We are a New People rising from the ruins of American empire."[15]

As Hayden himself should have recognized, however, extremism was leading the putative revolution to destroy itself. SDS, the core of student radicalism, had grown rapidly during these years, but even in 1969 it had only some 7,000 dues-paying national members and perhaps 30,000 followers in its local chapters. Events soon proved that it was both too large to maintain internal coherence and too small to avoid the personal intensity of internal conflict. Part of its problem could be traced back to its reluctance, born of its distaste for the dogmatism of the Old Left, to form a detailed ideology for itself. Although SDS clung to its vision of a participatory democracy in which the people directly controlled their institutions, it had not worked out a systematic analysis that could tell it how to get to that ideal. This disposition suited the progressive outlook of its founding years, when it was assumed that the right ideas would develop out of the effort to solve social problems, but the tense and increasingly dogmatic late sixties created conditions for the resurgence of ideology, a need for articles of faith that could explain the world of dark turbulence that had appeared. And the only ideology available to the New Left was that of the Old Left: namely, Marxism. It received a special boost from the popularity among the young of Herbert Marcuse, a veteran leftist who combined Marxian class analysis with Freudian ideas about sex. The sixty-year-old Marcuse, among the oldest of the numerous older prophets of a new order who sprang up in the 1960s, hoped to inspire youth with the idea of overthrowing a repressive social order that had denied them happiness.

The triumph of Marxism within SDS was assured by the efforts of the Progressive Labor (PL) Party—a small Marxist youth organization. Although PL members were only a minority, SDS was susceptible to the influence of their Marxian views. SDSers who had cared little about Marx before, recalled one member, "became 'Marxists' overnight."[16] As a result, the organization fell victim to an Old Left disease of factional conflict fueled by dogmatic disputes over the meaning of Marxism, a problem further complicated by tensions between black and white radicals.

In 1969, SDS was split between its PL members, who clung to orthodox Marxism, and a "Third World" faction, which looked to the more romantic, guerrilla war-oriented Marxism associated with Cuba and Vietnam. This second faction, known as the Weathermen, drew much of its strength from the masses of young enthusiasts who had joined SDS in the mid-1960s. Generally from the Midwest or Southwest, they saw themselves as authentic American radicals freed from the constraints of imported dogmas. When SDS held its annual national convention in Chicago, the Third Worlders attempted to win over uncommitted members by circulating a paper titled from a Bob Dylan song, "You Don't Need a Weatherman to Know Which Way the Wind Blows." Despite this use of a popular song and despite the support of the Black Panthers, the Weathermen could not win the control they wanted and bolted from the convention, dealing the organization a shattering blow from which it never recovered.

Although the PL faction gained control of the rump organization, public attention went with the Weathermen. They dreamed of becoming guerrilla fighters who would live in a sea of increasing popular support furnished by the disadvantaged and oppressed. Believing that they could win the support of poor and working-class youth by proving how tough they were, they went on a rampage of violence, trashing hamburger stands and other teenage hangouts and bursting into schools, where they beat up a few teachers, daring the kids to join them in their campaign of "kicking ass" and "getting us a few pigs." They made few converts. In Ann Arbor, one group of Weathermen picked a fight with a motorcycle gang and got bloodied without winning the respect of the gang. They desperately wanted to join forces with the Black Panthers but got their reply from Illinois Panther leader Fred Hampton, who called one of their leaders a "motherfucking masochist" before knocking him to the ground.[17]

This guerrilla theater reached a saddening absurdity in October 1969 when the Weathermen assembled in Chicago to perpetrate their "Days of Rage," a planned payback for the attacks by the Chicago police on demonstrators the year before. Expecting to rally thousands of "anti-imperialist street fighters" to the attack, they managed to muster only a few hundred. Nevertheless, armored in white motorcycle helmets, they launched an assault on an assembled mass of some 2,000 police, who proceeded to shoot six of them and to beat up most of the rest. After that, the Weathermen went underground, but the grisly farce continued. In March 1970 a group of them were busy assembling bombs in a New York townhouse when their materials blew up in one great explosion; three died, and the rest fled. One of those who escaped was Kathy Boudin, the daughter of the prominent radical lawyer who had taken on the Indiana University case in 1963. She succeeded in remaining underground until 1981, when she and two other Weathermen killed three men in an armored car robbery and were sentenced to long prison terms. So ended the career of a young woman whom her father had proudly described in 1971 as having "devoted herself to the betterment of her fellow men."[18]

The Weathermen marked the end of SDS and of organized student radicalism. By venturing so far and so absurdly into the badlands of guerrilla warfare, radical students had only deepened public concerns about law and order while demonstrating that they were no match for law enforcement in the violence business. That lesson was taught with special brutality when the Chicago police killed Black Panther leader Fred Hampton in his apartment not long after Hampton had sneered at the Days of Rage as "Custeristic." Violence showed yet another ugly face when the hippie-like Charles Manson and his "family" committed a set of grisly murders in the Los Angeles area, producing a public reaction that led some of the "real" hippies to complain that "Manson, not a hippie at all, but a crazy ex-con, has fucked it up for everybody."[19]

Meanwhile, tensions were beginning to ease on campus. University administrators had accumulated enough experience and caution to manage student demands for change. The elimination of ROTC programs, greater freedom from the *in loco parentis* doctrine, provisions for student input on university decisions, and modifications of curricula reduced internal tensions by making for a more democratic campus. At the same time, several external changes promised to withdraw the war from the students' doorstep. The efforts of the Nixon administration to de-escalate the Vietnam conflict, changes in the draft laws, and the continued growth in the pool of eligible young men substantially lowered the chance that students would be drafted, while the steady rise of antiwar sentiment in all age groups increased hopes that the war could soon be brought to an end by peaceful means.

At the end of April 1970, however, President Nixon shocked hopes for disengagement by ordering an invasion of Cambodia. Within days, antiwar sentiment exploded on hundreds of campuses, resulting chiefly in student protest strikes but also in some violence. At Kent State University in Ohio, for instance, after students burned down the ROTC building, new efforts to suppress violence led to conflict which in turn flared briefly into war when National Guardsmen fired into a group of protesting students, killing four and wounding nine. Ten days later a student protest at Jackson State College in Mississippi ended in the death of two students and the wounding of twelve others when police fired into a dormitory. These killings ignited an even broader storm of protest throughout the country. An estimated thirty ROTC buildings were bombed or burned, and classes at some 500 colleges and universities were canceled, many for the rest of the semester.

Even so, it was evident that the majority of the young activists, far from becoming revolutionaries, were beginning to return to the political system. May 1970 brought at least two new student organizations dedicated to political action. One, the Movement for a New Congress, was formed at Princeton University to organize student support for the election of antiwar congressional candidates in the fall elections; soon thereafter, representatives from sixty colleges in the New York metropolitan area met at Columbia University and launched a campaign to elect antiwar congressmen from that area. Also in May, Sam Brown, the youth coordinator for the Gene McCarthy campaign in 1968, and Mike Brewer of the Ripon Society (a liberal Republican group) organized Project Pursestring to try to persuade Congress to cut off funds for the war; it soon claimed support on 100 campuses.

The summer of 1970 brought new reasons for student withdrawal from violence to politics. In August, the bombing of the Army Mathematics Research Center at the University of Wisconsin killed one student. In the same month, Robert S. Starobin, a brilliant young historian and radical, itemized the weapons he had accumulated in preparation for some kind of conflict but confessed, "I still can't figure out under what circumstances to use them."[20] Shortly after that, he turned one of the guns on himself, ending his life.

In 1969–70 the percentage of students who called themselves radicals peaked at approximately 14 percent and then fell to less than 10 percent before the end of 1970. Although nearly two-thirds of students in 1970 believed that campus radicalism would grow, the proportion declined to one-third a year later. And whereas in 1970 there seemed reason to fear what a university president called "an unprecedented alienation of American youth," one poll in 1971 indicated that some 87 percent of the young accepted the principle that children should respect their parents—hardly a sign of widespread alienation.[21]

Even the veteran radical Tom Hayden began to have second thoughts about his revolutionary passions. In 1972, soon after a court overturned his five-year prison sentence for his part in the Chicago demonstrations, Hayden began to move into politics, involving himself in the Indochina Peace Campaign organized earlier that year. This step, he said later, was motivated both by new possibilities for peaceful change and by his feeling that "we had gotten ourselves isolated by being anticountry, antiflag, antieverything." The aim of the campaign was to rally opposition to spending for the war. Hayden and his future wife, Jane Fonda, were the stars of the effort, giving him, he later recalled, "a sense of excitement about finally being accepted, fitting into the mainstream."[22]

Hayden and other returning radicals segregated themselves from the conventional two-party system, but even they, along with thousands of other young Americans who were less radical, were heartened by the changes occurring within the Democratic Party. After their 1968 debacle, the Democrats adopted a set of rules opening the party to considerably greater influence from blacks, women, and the young at the expense of the old-line politicians who had dominated the 1968 convention. It was an opportunity made to order for Senator George McGovern, a South Dakota preacher's son, who appealed strongly to the moral sensibilities of liberal-minded youth. McGovern identified himself with opposition to the Vietnam War, with amnesty for those who had refused to serve in the war, and with racial justice as well as with such cultural issues as the liberalization of laws against abortion and marijuana.

McGovern's aides were able to put together a strong primary campaign organization manned by thousands of students under the generalship of thirty-four-year-old Gary Hart of Colorado. To emphasize the importance of youth, McGovern's campaign coordinator in New York was a twenty-year-old Columbia University student, and in Iowa it was a twenty-five-year-old former supporter of Eugene McCarthy. The campaign concentrated principally on college students, but some effort was made to attract non-college youth as well. Supported by his army of student volunteers, McGovern was able to build a commanding lead for the Democratic presidential nomination.

At the nominating convention the young appeared in unprecedented numbers. Delegates under thirty made up 23 percent of the delegates, as opposed to less than 3 percent in 1968. With the aid of the increased number of blacks and women selected under the new rules, the old party leadership was pushed aside, the party platform was liberalized, and McGovern was nominated. In accepting the nomination, he predicted "a new period of important and hopeful changes in America," promised to withdraw all American troops from Vietnam within ninety days after he became president, and urged all Americans to "come home to the belief that we can seek a better world."[23]

McGovern's nomination to run against the Republican Richard Nixon made the election of 1972 potentially the closest thing in American history to a contest between generations and fundamental political philosophies. Ralph J. Gleason, editor of *Rolling Stone*, proclaimed it a politicized rerun "of the Great Rock & Roll debate" that had begun in the 1950s, to be won by the music of the young. The new music had educated the new generation to new political perceptions: "Every rock record that you ever liked was a step toward defeating Richard Milhous Nixon." Even without the support of the leaders of the Establishment, Gleason predicted, McGovern could win by drawing on the "huge energy potential" of 25 million new voters.[24] Attempting a more scholarly effort to measure the influence of youth in politics, Sydney Hyman estimated that as many as 32 million first-time voters under twenty-six might vote, but he wondered whether many would actually do so, noting that students often were activated to political involvements by dramatic events but had trouble concentrating on the normal political activities that produced results.

The primary campaign had been well managed; however, the election campaign was a disaster marked by McGovern's hesitations and uncertainties over his vice-presidential running mate, Thomas Eagleton (who was eventually forced to retire from the ticket after it was discovered that he had been treated for severe psychological depression), and also over his stance on some of the issues. After having broached a startling new proposal for the use of the tax system to transfer wealth from the rich to the poor, for example, McGovern dampened the enthusiasm of radicals and others by softening his position. Because of this and his cautiousness on abortion and other cultural issues, radicals such as Tom Hayden either gave him lukewarm support or looked elsewhere.

Some found their ideal candidate in the godparent of the baby-boom generation, Dr. Benjamin Spock. After having advised parents on child-raising for decades, Spock joined the peace movement in the early 1960s, and was radicalized by the escalation of the war in Vietnam. In late 1971 he accepted the presidential nomination of the newly formed People's Party. A month before the election, he criticized McGovern for accepting "the existing free enterprise system" and declared that industry should be forced to abandon its preoccupation with profit in favor of respect for the environment and for workers. He endorsed his party's opposition to all laws creating "crimes" without victims, such as the laws against marijuana, and also its proposals for both a minimum guaranteed income and a maximum income to ensure that all Americans had a share of prosperity. He gave his greatest enthusiasm to a scheme to decentralize control of industry into boards representing workers, consumers, and the public interest, with a corresponding decentralization of all government to ensure direct popular control of public services: "A basic sickness of our society is the conviction of millions of citizens that they are impotent pawns of a dehumanized and dehumanizing system."[25] It was participatory democracy with a vengeance.

While the political left divided between McGovern's liberalism and Spock's radicalism, the forces of conservatism, split in 1968, were largely reunited, thanks to an assassination attempt that put presidential contender George Wallace in the hospital and out of the race. And conservatism was strengthened by the radical rhetoric of some of the young. Lacking any real understanding of politics and government, some young rebels continued to indulge in attacks on the System and in calls for revolution, convincing many anxious voters that indeed a crisis of order demanded some strong leader who could override the effects of permissiveness on youth. During the previous two years, Republicans had mounted a campaign claiming that permissive child-rearing and permissive liberal policies were responsible for rebellious youth. In California, Governor Ronald Reagan had used the charge to great effect, leading one Democrat to complain that apparently "if your kid goes wrong its the fault of permissive Democrats. It's like the kids were dropped off at Democratic headquarters at birth and reared by Dr. Spock to do everything wrong."[26] Along with the race issue, the issue of permissiveness served to weaken what had been the Democratic grip on the South, where traditionalism and reverence for authority were especially strong.

By October the polls indicated that incumbent President Nixon had a commanding lead among voters generally. The only real uncertainty concerned the political behavior of the young, which way they would vote or whether they would vote at all. Senator Edward Kennedy estimated that the lowering of the voting age had added 11 million potential new voters to the 14 million who had turned twenty-one since the last election. These 25 million, Kennedy hoped, would "bring new men and new ideas and new realities in our political life," though he had to admit that young Americans in the past had been the least likely to vote.[27]

Expectations of a high turnout were bolstered by an intense bipartisan competition for the youth vote. McGovern's aides intended to deploy 100,000 young volunteers to organize and register the young for voting, and by September they were employing sixty paid full-time coordinators to guide young volunteers in this campaign; the major focus was on the nation's nearly 6 million college students. The Nixon campaign organizers gave some attention to the campuses but, perceiving that college students were generally against the president, concentrated their attention on the 14 million young workers, many of whom had been well disposed toward George Wallace until he was forced from the race.

Despite the hopes of McGovern's supporters, every poll indicated that the young were not much different from their parents. Like them, younger voters preferred to give the incumbent president a chance to fulfill his promise to end the war with dignity rather than risk the untried radicalism of an untested leader. One of the greatest shocks to Democratic hopes came from a national survey of 100,000 high school students in early October, which revealed that they preferred Nixon over McGovern by more than 2 to 1—an ominous sign of which direction the second-wave baby boomers born after 1952 were likely to take. McGovern did much better with college students, but even there, his strength tended to be concentrated on the major campuses and among older students most affected by the radicalism of the sixties. Writing shortly before the election, Pat Caddell, the campaign's twenty-two-year-old chief pollster, concluded that the candidate was in trouble even with the young: although his hero was more in tune with the life-styles supposedly favored by youth, many young people proved not to be significantly different from older people in their life-styles. And youth culture itself certainly was no guarantee of support, since that culture tended to be indifferent to politics, its devotees responsive—if at all—to dramatic events rather than to basic issues.

The actual results of the November election simply confirmed what most observers had expected. McGovern won most student votes at major campuses (more than 75 percent at the University of Wisconsin, a center of student radicalism), but he barely edged out Nixon among young voters generally, and less than half of the young actually bothered to vote. The hoped-for new politics proved to be far more like the old politics, meting out the usual reward of daring innovation: a disastrous defeat. McGovern did receive more than 29 million votes (while People's Party candidate Benjamin Spock got only 78,801), but that was barely 38 percent of the largest vote ever cast in a presidential year. Nixon won reelection by a landslide throughout the country.

What had happened? Some observers blamed McGovern for running an inept campaign or for having antagonized the old politicians of his party or for simply being George McGovern, but the chances are that whatever he did he was doomed to be swamped by an incoming tide of conservatism. Bo Burlingham, the managing editor of *Ramparts* (a leading periodical of the cultural revolution), said that McGovern had staked his and the nation's future on a program drawn from the idealism of the sixties, but that idealism had already passed: "The sensibility of Americans—stretched to their limits in the 1960s—has now snapped back with a mean and reactionary vengence."[28] Indeed, there seems little doubt that the election registered a major shift favorable to conservatism in America, due in no small part to the law-and-order concerns raised by the militancy and extremism of radicals both white and black.

McGovern's defeat deepened the disillusion of democracy's children with politics, which had begun in the mid-1960s. Only an extreme revolutionary and hippie minority were prepared to dismiss a hopelessly racist, imperialistic, war-mongering, and morally corrupt Amerika, but many others found reason to believe that government, even liberal government, was discouragingly unlikely to change. The discontents of African Americans, the ugly realities of the war and the draft, and the heavy-handed suppression of antiwar protest indicated a betrayal of basic public ideals. And the democratic process by which these ideals could be retrieved had failed. Alongside the assassinations of such leaders as Robert Kennedy and Martin Luther King, the political process had produced a Lyndon Johnson, who had betrayed his promise of peace, and a Richard Nixon, who less than two years after his triumphant reelection in 1972 would be forced to resign because of his involvement in the Watergate scandals.

The young returned to society, then, with little but their disillusionment, without anything like a coherent ideology to guide and sustain them. Having learned their democratic commitments from their parents, they had become heavy consumers of ideas derived from the older generation, from people such as C. Wright Mills, Timothy Leary, Paul Goodman, Norman Mailer, the Beats, progressive educators, Marxists, anarchists, and even older generations of American radicals and visionaries. Democracy's children, probably the most literate generation ever produced in America, had learned from their reading the stuff from which to make manifestos. In the end, they ran this inheritance into the ground, leaving little basis for radical social thought and political action other than an outmoded Marxism.

Their younger brothers and sisters of the second wave, the products of the different circumstances of the 1950s, had even less to offer when they came of age. Democratic idealism did not entirely disappear, but it tended to reflect the overall disillusionment with the nation and its institutions. In place of strivings to affect a general improvement in the nation, the new generation substituted concern for and loyalty to the particular group, not only their own group but also blacks, women, and any others who could be seen as victims of society. If the sixties had brought hopes for fundamental democratic changes in the nation, the seventies saw increasing efforts of such groups and their supporters to pressure society into granting what they believed were *their* just rights and privileges. For a generation reared to affluence and subjected to disillusioning times, it did not seem unnatural to demand that America deliver its benefits with little thought of a return. And so, with occasional flashes of its old idealism, the new generation lapsed into a mood where self was far more important than social concerns.

NOTES

1. Harold W. Bernard, *Adolescent Development* (New York, 1957), 547–48.

2. John McDermott, "Thoughts on the Movement," in Priscilla Long, ed., *The New Left* (Boston, 1969), 32–13.

3. David Cortright, "The Greening of the Green," *Liberation* (Spring 1971): 51–52; and Cortright, *Soldiers in Revolt* (Garden City, NY, 1975), 3, 11, 14, 21.

4. Arthur Schlesinger Jr., "The New Liberal Coalition," *Progressive* 31 (1967): 15–19.

5. Theodore White, *The Making of the President—1968* (New York, 1969), 81, 87–88; Viorst, *Fire in the Streets*, 405, 409, 413.

6. Richard N. Goodwin, *Remembering America* (Boston, 1988), 495–98, 527–28; White, *Making of the President*, 88–89.

7. Jerry Rubin, "A Yippie Manifesto" in Leo Hamalian and Frederick R. Kail, eds., *The Radical Vision* (New York, 1970), 15; Rubin, *Growing [Up]*, 81–82.

8. Abbie Hoffman, *Revolution for the Hell of It* (New York, 1968), 102.

9. White, *Making of the President*, 297–98.

10. Libarle and Seligson, *High School Revolutionaries*, 8–10.

11. Alexander Bloom and Wini Breines, eds., *"Taking It to the Streets": A Sixties Reader* (New York, 1995), 323.

12. Hayden, "The Trial," 10–12.

13. Richard Hofstader, "The Future of American Violence," *Harper's Magazine* (April 1970): 47; Todd Gitlin, *The Sixties* (New York, 1987), 285.

14. Libarle and Seligson, *High School Revolutionaries*, 111–12, 232.

15. Jose Yglesias, "Right On with the Young Lords," in David Goldfield and James Lane, eds., *The Enduring Ghetto* (Philadelphia, 1973), 215; Hayden, "The Trial," 52.

16. Paul Glussman, "One, Two, Three . . . Many SDSs," *Ramparts* 8 (1968), 8; Gitlin, *Sixties*, 383.

17. Gitlin, *Sixties*, 391–94.

18. Peter Joseph, ed., *Good Times: An Oral History of the 1960s* (New York, 1973), 417–18.

19. Marshall Singer, "Fragments from the Shooting Gallery," *Ramparts* (April 1970): 18.

20. Julius Lester, "On the Suicide of a Revolutionary," *Liberation* (Spring 1971): 65–66.

21. Fred M. Hechinger and Grace Hechinger, *Growing Up in America* (New York, 1975), 403; Howard Junker, "The Apocalypse of Our Time Is Over," *Rolling Stone* (February 13, 1971): 43–47.

22. Paul Booth, "The Left Has Outgrown Its Aimless Period," *Progressive* (December 1971): 65–66; Miller, *Democracy*, 318–19; Zaroulis and Sullivan, *Who Spoke Up?*, 393–94.

23. White, *Making of the President*, 187–88; George McGovern, "American Politics Will Never Be the Same Again," *U.S. News & World Report* (July 24, 1972): 84–87.

24. *Rolling Stone* (August 17, 1972), 28.

25. Benjamin Spock, "An Open Letter to George McGovern," *Progressive* (October 1972): 42–44.

26. *New York Times* (May 19, 1972).

27. Edward M. Kennedy, "The Future Is Now for the 18-Year-Old Vote," *School and Society* 100 (1972): 151–55.

28. Bo Burlingham, "Who Really Lost the Election?" *Ramparts* (January 1973): 8–9.

CHAPTER **Ten**

CHANGE AND ITS LIMITS

G IVEN THE SIZE OF THE FORTIES GENERATION AND THE POWER OF
its experiences, its advance into maturity seemed certain to have
a significant effect on society and the future. The late 1960s
brought so persistent a use of the word "revolution" that, like much else,
the word was soon run into the ground. Change, yes, but what kind?
Old-fashioned wisdom had often looked upon the young as a horde of
barbarians yet to be civilized; in this case, it saw a massive and rebellious
barbarian army that might indeed overthrow the civilization its members
seemed unwilling to accept. Even Paul Goodman, who a decade before
had looked hopefully on his "crazy young allies," came at the very end of
the sixties to wonder about their disposition. Although he continued to
believe that youth ran "the only game in town" worth playing, he complained that too often "they do not sound like Isaac Newton, more a mob
of monkeys."[1]

The hesitations and reservations of the wise, however, were overshadowed in the early 1970s by a last rush of predictions that the young would
in the end redeem society. With the failure of radical politics, the hopes
for fundamental change came to depend on cultural revolution, the transformation of social values by the maturing young, as if the very youth of
the new generation were an embodiment of new values. One enthusiast
dreamed that the young were developing a new postindustrial "Dionysian"

141

personality that, as it gained influence in society, would end war, promote social welfare and the improvement of the environment, redistribute wealth, and effect other miracles of radical policy. "Within about fifteen years, we will see the first of the second-generation Dionysians," he predicted. "Drugs, sex, and personal styles will be more of a bore than a shock. They will expect warm and meaningful relations with others."[2] And so the old uptight society would melt away into a new society of freedom and love.

This hope for a fundamental cultural transformation was temporarily popularized in the early 1970s by Charles Reich in *The Greening of America*. Reich latched onto the concept of "consciousness," then often associated with psychedelic drugs, to argue that postindustrial American youth was introducing a new awareness and understanding of life destined to reshape all institutions and behavior. This Consciousness III— versus the Consciousness II of the older generation—placed the welfare of every individual above social institutions, respecting each person's individuality, though also holding to the ideal of human brotherhood. In part because of the effects of drugs in enhancing awareness, the Consciousness III person was able to acquire new knowledge without study or thought: "It might take a Consciousness II person twenty years of reading radical literature to 'know' that law is a tool of oppression; the young drug user just plain 'knows' it." This kind of reasoning led Reich to conclude that a revolutionizing new consciousness, begun with the appearance of the hippies, was spreading rapidly with the assistance of rock music and television. "When, in the fall of 1969, the courtyard of the Yale Law School," wrote this instructor at the school, "became for a few weeks the site of a commune, with tents, sleeping bags, and outdoor cooking, who could any longer doubt the clearing wind was coming?"[3]

Like many other books of prophecy, *The Greening of America* was a mix of acute observation and fatuous fantasy, but whatever its limitations, it was certainly one of the most popular and often quoted books of its time. Where politics had disappointed hopes for a fundamentally better world, it declared consciousness stronger than politics, for culture— the system of popular beliefs about the world—"controls the economic and political machine, not vice versa."[4] This pop version of philosophical idealism suited the anti-authoritarian and anti-intellectual temper of the counterculture. Whatever the strength of the existing power system and whatever the purported truths of reason, the new awareness would, with the growing influence of the new generation, ultimately transform all systems and determine all truths.

Reich's book reflected a widespread yearning in tune with the dwindling idealism of its times. If nothing else, the counterculture was a powerful negation, a rejection of established values and institutions that seemingly stood in the way of real happiness and virtue. For someone like John Sinclair, manager of the Detroit rock band MC5, the rock and roll music so popular with the young—and so despised by older generations— would be a powerful weapon of cultural revolution: "People have got to get it together, not part. People are now stuck in bullshit jobs, bullshit schools, bullshit houses, bullshit marriages, bullshit social and economic scenes."[5] Having been conditioned by their experience to view affluence as part of the natural order of things, the young rebels could reject what was called, in derision rather than pride, the American Way for its apparent fixation on consumerism. Morally, this rejection included the old faith in hard work as the way to success and with it much of the self-denial and self-discipline that the older generation has preached and at least occasionally practiced. Philosophically, the counterculture challenged modern civilization, condemning science and reason as the source of modern evil. Looking for understanding, many of the young rejected science in favor of such things as astrology and magic, where they hoped to rediscover some ancient tradition of wisdom that had been obscured by modern rationality.

This antimodern attitude helped form and animate the environmentalist movement, which became one of the great hopes for change in the 1970s. There was nothing new about environmental concerns. Democracy's children had learned about chemical pollution from their reading of such books as Rachel Carson's *Silent Spring* (1966), whose warnings against the use of DDT and other dangerous substances were reported in, among many other places, *Senior Scholastic*, where young readers were alerted that all of us are "now storing up poisons in our bodies." The growing hostility to modernity in the late 1960s, however, gave a radical twist to such concerns, making them a popular form of youth protest that helped produce the first Earth Day in April 1970, a kind of environmental Woodstock. Earth Day was especially the work of Denis Hayes (born in 1944), who quit Harvard Law School to organize it under the slogan "Earth—love it or leave it."[6]

Understandably, much of the movement was negative, featuring hostility to corporate bigness, nuclear power, processed foods, and large-scale mining and timber cutting. Occasionally, radical environmentalists resorted to the confrontational tactics of the past, including some violence from "eco-saboteurs" and environmental guerrillas who destroyed billboards and power lines and attempted to obstruct lumbering by spiking trees. Environmentalism also provided a rationale for rejecting the procreation ethic that had produced the baby boom, promoting the idea of zero population growth to reduce the exploitation of nature—"make love, not babies." More positively, they promoted the ideal of maintaining an ecological balance designed to benefit all living things from humans down to the smallest creature, all inhabitants of a common Earth. In 1974, Peter Berg, a former Digger, established the Planet Drum Foundation to promote the idea of "bio-regionalism," regional communities that would care for their own distinctive ecological systems, each the home of the tiniest plants and animals as well as of humankind.[7]

Environmentalism provided what was perhaps the broadest basis for the counterculture rebellion against modernity. It could not, however, sustain the counterculture. During the 1970s, cultural ferment lost its fizz, and the rebellion disintegrated into myriads of fragments. Religion combined with more secular strivings to produce one set of fragments in the form of "alternative" communities. Although the vast majority of hippie communes had disappeared by the mid-1970s, a few, especially those with some religious base, survived as miniature worlds set apart from the larger society. Among them was The Farm, a rural commune established in 1971 in southern Tennessee by a large group of migrants from the San Francisco Bay area. By the early 1980s it had become a thriving community, forming what its leader, Stephen Gaskin, called "a third world nation surrounded by the United States," a community that he believed was evolving alternatives to modern technology, methods suited to the needs of developing nations.[8] The continued existence of several dozen such communities offered hope for the creation of a new social and economic life conducive to the full development of human nature. In the words of the leaders of the Sirius Community in Massachusetts, they were the "builders of the dawn," harbingers of a new civilization.[9]

Political radicals looked to another form of cooperative life they called "action collectives," small groups formed for specific purposes. Mass demonstrations having failed, protesters organized local cooperatives to pool their power in fighting local wars against Establishment abuses. In New York City, for instance, one group founded in 1972 used street theater, sit-ins, and other tactics of the 1960s to compel the Honeywell Corporation to cease producing antipersonnel weapons. Collectives supported some of the remaining radical journals without resorting to circulation managers and other minions of the Establishment press. Especially popular were the many food cooperatives that purchased food in bulk, both to reduce costs and to provide the organic products not then available in supermarkets. All such groups suited the dream long promulgated by Paul Goodman and others of a radically decentralized world where grassroots power and activity would replace what a proponent called "the enforced passivity and alienation of everyday life."[10]

Cultural rebels also opened more individualistic paths toward self-satisfaction and development. In his *Growing (Up) at Thirty-Seven* (1976), former Yippie Jerry Rubin declared that he was participating in "the Inner Revolution of the 1970's," which was bringing what he called a spiritual rebirth to America: "We are looking for meaning in our life, pleasure in our bodies, and honest communication."[11] A decade later he was pursuing a more materialistic dream on Wall Street. For Rubin and many others, rebirth had less to do with spirit than with body. Seeking a way to good feeling and personal fulfillment, they turned to the human potential movement, which promised to enable the unfulfilled to "get in touch with their feelings" and otherwise discover the keys to a deeper and intenser life—encounter groups, sensitivity training, meditation, transactional analysis, yoga, breathing exercises, uninhibited sex, and whatever else seemed likely to lift the self out of its old confining ruts.

Those who participated in the human potential movement often reasoned that by becoming "self-actualizing" or "fully functioning" persons, they were helping to improve society without depending on the risky process of politics. If nothing else, they were learning to love themselves as they believed they should love others, thereby continuing the tradition of the "Love Generation." Having been brought up in an intensely psychological age, with its promise of liberating therapies, seekers were naturally drawn to this "gospel of self-fulfillment," as Philip Rieff termed it, the old romantic dream of human perfectibility mated to modern therapeutic techniques.[12] One of the more enduring results was a preoccupation with personal health, setting new records of interest in such physical matters as diet and exercise, organic foods, and aerobics.

The new generation gave great stress to the gratification of desire, especially sexual desire. Beginning in the sixties, the mass march of the generation through prolonged adolescence had accelerated the sexual revolution, which had been brewing even before Kinsey. The result by the seventies was a sexual libertarianism that sanctioned an active interest in nearly every aspect of sex. In August 1970 the *New York Times* bestseller list was headed by Dr. David Reuben's *Everything You Always Wanted to Know about Sex*; right behind it was *The Sensuous Woman*, written by "J," a former advertising copywriter. At its libertarian extreme

the new sexuality embraced recreational sex, group sex, and homosexuality—any act that produced pleasure without seeming to hurt anyone. According to an advertisement for the best-selling book *The Joy of Sex*
(subtitled "A Gourmet Guide to Love Making"), the book proved that
"there are no rules, as long as there is mutual pleasure—and that your
choices are virtually unlimited."[13] In 1973 the Kinsey Institute for Sexual
Research in Bloomington, Indiana, celebrated its twenty-fifth anniversary
by declaring that the United States was headed toward a new era of free
and open sexual behavior.

The same tolerance was given to drug use, at least in regard to marijuana. In 1971 the young delegates at the decennial White House Conference on Youth, hardly a radical group, passed resolutions calling for the
legalization of marijuana and for amnesty to those convicted of its use.
During these years the makers of Acapulco Gold, a popular rolling paper
for marijuana cigarettes, advertised in *Rolling Stone* that they were devoting all profits to a campaign to legalize grass; they headed their ad
with a carefully footnoted quotation from George Washington: "Make
the most of the India Hemp Seed and sow it everywhere."[14] Whereas in
1967 a Gallup poll indicated that only 5 percent of college students had
tried grass, in a 1972 poll the percentage had risen to 51. Three years
later a survey found that 26 percent of high school students and 41 percent of college students considered themselves regular drug users. By
the mid-1970s, drug addiction seemed to be spinning out of control, a
$17 billion-a-year habit and still growing.

Some continued to approve of these developments. In 1973, Timothy
Leary, the guru of drugs, proclaimed the advent of a Hedonic Age: "Western civilization is now moving beyond the mechanical age into the new
era of nonrepressed and experiential freedom." In these new times, where
work was being replaced by leisure, said Leary, the young were adopting
a "hedonic psychology" oriented toward the maximization of pleasure.[15]
The excesses of this self-centered search for pleasure, however, inevitably
provoked strong criticism of what Tom Wolfe called the Me Generation
with its self-centered indulgence. Eventually, a reaction would develop,
especially when, with maturity, the generation began to ponder some of
the consequences of unrestrained sexual license.

The drive for freedom and self-realization, however, had a more noble
and enduring side, most notably in a continued effort to realize the full-
ness of the values that democracy's children had learned from their parents in the 1940s. In 1968 the sociologist Herbert Gans caught a notable
truth in his essay "The 'Equality' Revolution"; he observed that the young

had identified themselves with a broad movement to bring freedom and opportunity to every class of Americans. Gans believed that the demand for freedom would take many forms, from greater participation in decision-making to greater individual autonomy.

The equality revolution was driven perhaps less by altruism than by self-interest, but if so, that only assured its broad and fundamental effect. At its most altruistic, it continued the earlier commitment to eliminating racial discrimination which democracy's children had learned from their parents, beginning with their early years in the 1940s. As older advocates of racial equality had hoped, the new generation seemed to have escaped from much of the racism that had long afflicted the nation, although numerous exceptions remained. "Equal rights for all races" was well on its way to becoming the reigning principle governing decision-making. More tangibly, the young supported and expanded the gains in racial relations which had been made since the 1950s, especially the elimination of the more obvious forms of segregation, the expansion of black political influence, and new employment opportunities. Two generations earlier, the white nation had accepted the systematic disfranchisement of most of its black population; in the 1970s it was electing a growing number of black mayors and representatives. And between 1959 and 1972 the proportion of nonwhite families with middle-class incomes or higher more than tripled, from 11 to 34 percent.

Much of this improvement was closely related to dramatic increases in educational opportunities for blacks. Under pressure from liberal-minded white students as well as blacks, many colleges adopted programs to expand the presence of nonwhites in higher education. At the top, this meant the appointment of more minority people to faculty positions and to college governing boards. Even more important was the increase in the number of nonwhite students, much of it the result of systematic recruitment. Reacting against the inadequacies of minority education, universities altered their admission standards. In New York City, after the once restrictive City University adopted an open admissions policy that accepted all city high school graduates regardless of grades, enrollments of nonwhite students more than doubled, from 14 to 33 percent. Nationally, the percentage of nonwhites who were college graduates increased from 5.4 in 1960 to over 12 percent in 1973.

These were some of the results of the longtime drive for racial justice which democracy's children had grown into since the 1940s. The new generation, however, added some significant new dimensions to the equality revolution which served to weaken as well as expand that drive, most notably in the competition of groups such as women, Native Americans, Hispanic Americans, and others who demanded justice for themselves. Although these groups were more sympathetic than not to the strivings of black Americans for equality, they did tend to dissipate what the head of the National Urban League, Vernon E. Jordan, called "the nation's sparse moral energies."[16]

The most significant competition came from women. In 1963, Betty Friedan published *The Feminine Mystique*, which helped break the charmed silence that had concealed the growing discontent of educated women with domesticity. Having completed their work as mothers, they now demanded the opportunity to have rewarding work outside the home. These generally older women were the leading force behind the founding in 1966 of the National Organization for Women (NOW), whose statement of purpose declared that "the time has come for a new movement toward true equality for all women in America and toward a fully equal partnership of the sexes."[17] The precipitant for its formation was a decision of the federal Equal Employment Opportunity Commission to exclude women from its 1963 and 1965 provisions against discrimination in hiring and wages. NOW retrieved the women's rights cause from its years of subordination to motherhood and family. Following the example of pre–Civil War feminists, it adopted an updated Woman's Bill of Rights demanding equal access to education and employment, maternity leaves and child day-care facilities for working women, acceptance of a woman's right to control her reproductive life, and protection against all forms of discrimination.

The new movement influenced every aspect of society. In politics, women intensified their demands for a significant role in the governing process and for a constitutional amendment banning discrimination on the basis of sex. From the 1960s on, they won a growing number of appointive and elective positions in government, locally and nationally. In all three major religions, they demanded that their "second-class citizenship" be ended, chiefly through the expansion of their ecclesiastical voting rights and their ordination as clerics: "Women's caucuses have been formed in virtually every major denomination," wrote a religious reporter in 1974, "and their leaders have lined up beside blacks, Mexican-Americans and youth in demanding more power."[18]

Along with power, women demanded and achieved greater career opportunities for college-educated women; the number of women entering law school, for instance, increased by 500 percent during the seventies. Advances in virtually every professional category explain why, in the face of much pessimism regarding employment, female college students were optimistic about their economic future. In part because of this growth in professional employment, the times saw a weakening of traditional gender distinctions in both work and play. Young husbands of professional women took on somewhat more household responsibility than their fathers had done: in 1984, a survey of baby boomers found that three-quarters of married men rejected old-style marriage in favor of an equal marriage in which the husband and wife shared income-earning work, homemaking, and child-raising.

Like other efforts to expand American democracy, the women's movement was complicated by the emergence of a radical form within it, a radical feminism headed by young women of the baby-boom generation. Many of these young women had been raised in democratic households where they had been viewed as having the same basic right to self-fulfillment as boys. Like their brothers, they had generally gone off to college, often to become involved in civil rights work and radical causes. And more than their brothers, they were outraged by the gap between their high expectations and social realities. Even within such organizations as SNCC and SDS, they came to conclude that they were being exploited by a male leadership that denied them fair and equal treatment. Although some young men appreciated their position, others rejected and ridiculed their expectations. In 1968, such experiences with "male chauvinism" drove many young women to participate in the women's liberation movement.

Radical feminism reflected the growing particulars that fragmented the radical movement. Where young black radicals turned to race pride and to demands for the overturn of a racist society, young women came to see themselves as the victims of an oppression as vicious as racism: namely, "sexism," which taught its victims to see themselves as inferior to their victimizers. They strove to raise a general "consciousness" of what one militant group, the Redstockings, called total oppression: "We are exploited as sex objects, breeders, domestic servants, and cheap labor. We are considered inferior beings, whose only purpose is to enhance men's lives." They demanded that sexism be ended and that the whole structure of male domination—virtually society itself—be dismantled. The enemy of women's liberation, wrote Muriel McClelland, "is a political ordering whereby half the human race rules the other half—whether we call this pattern patriarchy, male domination, male supremacy, chauvinism, whatever."[19]

Some radicals dreamed of creating an independent woman's world with cooperative child care and other elements of care for women, which they would control so that, free from male dominance and meddling, they could develop competence and self-confidence. They also hoped to overthrow the traditional gender roles that had governed their parents' lives, so that women could be accepted as breadwinners and power brokers and men as nurturers and homemakers, if that were the case. They sought a world of options where "assertive, competitive, and independent behavior should not be closed to women," said Joy Osofsky, and "dependent, passive and nurturant behaviors should not be closed to men."[20] In the collective that published the *Great Speckled Bird*, Atlanta's underground newspaper, women took on more of the roles of writers and business managers, while the men did more of the typing.

This feminine radicalism had begun to fade by the mid-1970s, weakened by differences over class and sexual issues, but the women's rights movement continued to be a powerful influence for a new democracy. Among other things, it called attention to much real injustice relating to women, and it helped create various new programs to serve their needs, including Women's Studies programs in the colleges. Over the decades following 1970 it forced a restructuring of business, sports, schools, government, and even the military to encourage equal opportunity and treatment. Its excesses raised strong male opposition, but it had the powerful support of both civil rights laws and the sense of fair play.

The women's movement was both reinforced and distracted by even more radical demands for empowerment in the realm of sex and gender, especially for public acceptance of various forms of transsexualism and transgenderism that defied traditional sterotypes. The most extreme were the growing number of "sexual reassignment" surgeries first brought to popular attention by Christine Jorgensen in the early 1970s, surgeries to release the "woman trapped in a man's body," ending decades of frustration.

Beginning in the 1970s, previously closeted and isolated transsexuals and transvestites formed what eventually became a network of organizations for their support and advancement. For the first time, those who did not fit conventional gender types were able to create a community of their own. Although most of these groups were primarily social, they also challenged the attitudes and restraints which they believed denied them the freedom to express their real selves. One primary aim was to overcome the popular belief that males who dressed as women were homosexual; in fact, the vast majority were heterosexual but needed to express a strong feminine side of their being. By redefining themselves as an oppressed minority rather than as a class of deviants, they were able to overturn laws against cross-dressing on the equal-rights grounds that they were not being allowed the same freedom as women to wear the clothing of the opposite sex.

Whatever their sexual orientation, the transgendered benefited from the successful striving of the far more numerous and influential community of homosexuals—who succeeded in getting society to accept their way of naming themselves, as "gays." The development of their movement roughly paralleled that of blacks and of women. In the mid-1960s, leadership in the hitherto secretive and isolated gay community had begun to organize a legal challenge against discrimination. Before long, this movement proved to be too slow for many of the impatient young. While older gays tended to cling to their traditional secrecy, their young compatriots on college campuses often "came out of the closet" openly and aggressively to demand equal rights for themselves not only before the law but against police harassment. Like heterosexual radicals, they began to protest the traditional hassling practices of the "pigs," and on June 27, 1969, they fought back when the police raided a gay hangout in New York's Greenwich Village, the Stonewall Inn. This incident served as the Boston Tea Party of the gay community, helping to activate protests not only against police abuses but also against discrimination in jobs and housing.[21]

Gay Power became a reality with the formation of the Gay Liberation Front (GLF), a more open and aggressive organization than the cautious homophile groups of the past. Jim Fouratt, a hippie and one of the founders of GLF, found that when he called on his New Left friends to rally to the support of gays after Stonewall, virtually none of them showed up, because political radicals had little liking for "fags." Having to depend on themselves, he and other gays formed GLF in order to carry on a national fight for equal rights and for public acceptance. By the mid-1970s the gay community had become an open and influential force in many places, with more than 800 local organizations (in 1969, there had been only fifty), often with their own newspapers and services. Fighting the public tendency to label them as deviants, they sought acceptance within the democratic community as human beings whose worth was to be determined not by society's prejudices but by their own character and contributions. They believed that in doing so, they were fighting for the rights of all. In 1972, Boston's *Fag Rag*, part of a national network of gay newspapers, called for "self-government and self-determination of all peoples irrespective of national, sexual, party, race, age or other artificially imposed categories."[22]

The addition of sex and gender to the democratic agenda promised to expand the area of human freedom in the interest of self-fulfillment for all, raising the dream of a society in which the full diversity of the human race would be free to express itself, ending a fundamental cause of human misery and conflict. "The sociological truth," declared the *Journal of Male Feminism* in 1979, "is that we minorities are part of the most widespread movement of the human world today: the movement to cope with the excessive masculiness that has characterized the dominant class in modern civilization" and had been the source of war and the rest of the world's woes.[23] A champion of gay rights declared that to overcome moral prejudice in favor of equal rights would benefit human individuality in general and be a victory for the right of all persons to realize their essential selves. The new polydemocracy was the ideal of the democratic family writ large and in a radical way undreamed of thirty years before. The addition of blacks, women, gays, the transgendered, and other previously excluded groups to what had begun as the exclusive province of white males was truly a radical change, whose completion promised a radically better world.

Was this ideal in fact too radical ever to be completed? It was evident at the very beginning that the movement challenged powerful entrenched interests and equally powerful habits. In the long run, the basic question was whether victory would be won by an active minority aggressively expanding the limits of equality or by a more passive majority adhering to things as they were. Those who believed in the eventual triumph of the counterculture saw reason to believe that the future belonged to the venturesome minority. The ones who had questioned the American dream would be the ones to reshape it.

This was the governing assumption of Daniel Yankelovich when he wrote up the results of his 1973 survey of youth opinion under the title *The New Morality*. Yankelovich began by quoting his prediction of three years before that the new values held by student radicals would spread to all youth and eventually to the whole population: "At each stage in the process, a synthesis of old and new will finally be reached though the process may take decades and perhaps generations." He quoted his prediction in order to declare that he had been much too conservative in his time estimate, that what he had thought might take generations was already well under way.[24]

This conclusion rested largely on what appeared to be a rapidly growing acceptance of the new values—already seemingly accepted by college students—by the non-college majority of the youth population. When compared with a 1969 opinion survey, the new results seemed to confirm a widespread rejection of established institutions and ways. Significantly declining percentages of non-college youth affirmed the importance of religion (from 65 percent in 1969 to 42 percent in 1973), of a clean moral life (from 78 to 57 percent), of patriotism (from 61 to 40 percent), and of respect for authority, whether of bosses (71 to 57 percent) or the police (79 to 60 percent). At the same time, there was a notably greater emphasis on individual freedom particularly in matters sexual, extending even to abortion and homosexuality. These and other findings seemed to demonstrate that a fundamental moral change, if not a cultural revolution, was well under way in American society.

The trend was neither so simple nor so inexorable, however, in part because of fundamental differences between the forties generation and the second wave of the baby boom, born in the 1950s. During the late 1960s, expectations for radical change had been founded on the belief that the new generation was one great cohort that would grow more radical year by year. In fact, the young were better seen as members of two notably distinct subgenerations who were to have notably different impacts on society. In the 1980s, Annie Gottlieb, a member of the forties generation, gave her version of this difference: "While the 'first wave' people tend to be earnest, passionate, visionary, and somewhat shell-shocked, 'second-wavers' seem ironic and low key, with lower expectations yet greater resiliency."[25] In 1988 a student of baby-boom values found that a significantly greater portion of the first-wavers were "inner-directed," that is, governed more by definite internal values than were their younger brethren.

Whatever the exact nature of this difference, it was rooted in two distinct generational experiences. Most of the idealism that had fueled the youth rebellion belonged to those born in the 1940s and reared to pursue the ideal of the democratic family. In contrast, the second wave was subjected to the greater influence of the Cold War conservatism of the Eisenhower years and to television, with its aversion to print literacy and rationality. Moreover, members of the first wave were far more likely to be the oldest children in families and thus more likely than their younger siblings to have been exposed to the child-rearing ideals of democratic parents.

Reaching adolescence during the tumultuous 1960s, the younger ones had mixed feelings about the styles and behaviors of the radicals of the first wave. Probably many shared the feelings of nineteen-year-old Joyce

Maynard, who complained that she and her peers had been led to believe that they would share in the exciting times of their older siblings when they grew up, yet "now we can vote, and we're old enough to attend rallies, . . . and suddenly it doesn't seem to matter any more." Moreover, they had sacrificed much of their own adolescence: "My generation is special because of what we missed rather than what we got."[26] Others were willing to let the excitement pass. By 1974, college students were turning away from political activism to such practical concerns as preparing for a job. On campus, long hair and beards gave way to the clean look, and dreams of radical change gave way to what Nora Sayre called the new nostalgia, which led teenagers to revive the popular culture of the 1950s, those supposedly happy days from which the more intelligent first-wavers had been eager to escape: "Pony tails and Howdy Doody, old Elvis Presley ducktails and slow, wailing songs about loving forever, 'really and truly.' "[27] Probably that nostalgia was a factor in the strong support in the high schools for Nixon's reelection in 1972.

The result, then, was far less a cultural shift than had been either hoped or feared. A 1975 survey of drug usage, for instance, revealed that 58 percent of the young did not take drugs, because they believed either that the practice was morally wrong or that it would hurt them. Another survey of high school student leaders in the same year indicated significant declines in the percentage of those who favored the legalization of marijuana and those who accepted a man and woman's living together without marriage. Nearly one-third indicated that they had had sexual intercourse (nearly double the 1970 figure), but this proportion had not increased over the previous two years.

Although the new morality continued to be an influence, there were signs by the mid-1970s that the moral order was beginning to settle down. This outcome had been predicted in 1971 by Peter Drucker, the sanest and most consistently correct of those who tried to read the social trends of the times. Regarding Consciousness III, Drucker observed that what people like Reich presumed to be the wave of the future was simply a youth culture sustained by annual large crops of rebellious adolescents, but that adolescents eventually become young adults who "tend to be the most conventional group of the population," since they are the ones who must confront the problems of finding work, establishing homes, and raising families. He concluded that such struggles would dampen the social and cultural enthusiasms of the young and would instill in them much of the "grubby materialism" that they had denounced in their parents.[28] By the middle of the decade, this process was well under way.

Indeed, the great accomplishment of the otherwise unaccomplished 1970s may have been to provide for the social absorption of the young masses without a fundamental disruption of American life. Most of the many who had abandoned society, psychologically as well as physically, came home. They often brought with them the attitudes and hopes of the 1960s, but most of them eventually came to terms with the conventions of the established world. There would be change, but much of it would be in a conservative direction.

NOTES

1. Paul Goodman, *The New Reformation* (New York, 1970), xii–xiii.
2. Lauren Langmen, "Dionysius—Child of Tomorrow," in David Gottlieb, ed., *Youth in Contemporary Society* (Beverly Hills, CA, 1973), 137–46.
3. Charles A. Reich, *The Greening of America* (New York, 1970), 225–26, 261, 394.
4. Ibid., 306.
5. Bloom and Breines, *Taking It to the Streets*, 303.
6. "The Furor over Pesticides," *Senior Scholastic* 81 (1962–63): 10–12; David DeLeon, *Leaders from the 1960s* (Westport, CT, 1994), 327.
7. Chepesiuk, *Sixties Radicals*, 118–19; Richard Todd, "Psychic Farming," *Atlantic Monthly* (April 1973): 114–20.
8. Oliver Popenoe and Cris Popenoe, *Seeds of Tomorrow* (San Francisco, 1981), 91.
9. Corrine McLaughlin and Gordon Davidson, *Builders of the Dawn* (Walpole, NH, 1985).
10. *Liberation* (August 1972): 3–4; Raymond Mungo, *Cosmic Profit: How to Make Money without Doing Time* (Boston, 1979), xiv.
11. Rubin, *Growing [Up]*, 91, 199–201, and Rubin, "From the Streets to the Body," *Psychology Today* (September 1973): 70–71.
12. Eleanor Criswell and Severin Peterson, "The Whole Soul Catalogue," *Psychology Today* (April 1972): 57.
13. *New York Times* (May 21, 1970): 40; (August 15, 1970): 28.
14. *Rolling Stone* (May 27, 1971): 1; (March 16, 1972): 28.
15. Timothy Leary, "The Principles and Practice of Hedonic Psychology," *Psychology Today* (January 1973): 53–58.
16. Vernon E. Jordan, "End of the Second Reconstruction," *Vital Speeches* 38 (1971–72): 31–34.
17. "The National Organization for Women," in Cynthia Fuchs Epstein and William J. Goode, eds., *The Other Half* (Englewood Cliffs, NJ, 1971), 193.
18. Betty Yorburg, "The New Women's Movement," *Intellect* 103 (1974–75): 100–102; Jo Freeman, "The Politics of Woman's Liberation," *Intellect* 103 (1974–75): 469.
19. "Redstockings Manifesto," in Epstein and Goode, *Other Half*, 199–201.

20. Yorburg, "New Women's Movement," 101–2.

21. Allen Young, "Out of the Closet: A Gay Manifesto," *Ramparts* (November 1971): 52.

22. Wachsberger, *Voices*, 1:202–3.

23. John T. Talamine, *Boys Will Be Girls: The Hidden World of the Heterosexual Male Transvestite* (Lanham, MD, 1982), 55.

24. Daniel Yankelovich, *The New Morality* (New York, 1974), 10–11.

25. Annie Gottlieb, *Do You Believe in Magic? The Second Coming of the Sixties* (New York, 1974), 10.

26. Joyce Maynard, *Looking Back: A Chronicle of Growing Up Old in the Sixties* (Garden City, NY, 1973), 6.

27. Nora Sayre, "The New Nostalgia," *Progressive* 36 (1972): 38.

28. Peter Drucker, "The Surprising Seventies," *Harper's Magazine* (July 1971): 35–37.

CHAPTER **Eleven**

COMING HOME

B Y THE EARLY 1970S ALL OF THE FORTIES GENERATION, THE FIRST
wave of baby boomers, had reached age twenty-one or more; indeed, the older and often more radical members were approaching
age thirty, beyond which lay the dark beginnings of something called middle
age. Never again would they experience life so vividly or live life so freely.
Like it or not, however, an irresistible force impelled them toward adulthood and toward a place in society. Although this prospect inspired reports of increased suicide, alcoholism, and psychological problems, the
majority response was, if not entirely positive, at least less dire.

As early as 1970 the dread passage came to Jack Weinberg, who some
years before at Berkeley had raised the rallying cry, "Don't trust anyone
over thirty." Having himself reached that age, he had changed his mind.
Though still active in radical causes, he had concluded that the advances
he wanted could not be accomplished by the young alone. In 1974, *Rolling Stone* queried thirty-four of the first baby boomers to reach thirty and
found that for most of them it was no big deal. One of them had planned
to celebrate her thirtieth birthday with a "psychic death" to be attained
by taking psychedelic drugs—only to become sick with the flu. Mundane
reality quietly did its work on all but the dead; among those who escaped
by way of death was the great rock singer Janis Joplin, the victim of a
drug overdose in the fall of 1970 at age twenty-seven.

Some did try to fend off maturity by staying out of society. A handful of the Weathermen remained militantly in exile but eventually dribbled back. In 1970, after his girlfriend was killed by a botched bomb blast, Bill Ayres went underground with his future wife, Bernadine Dohrn; a decade later the two turned themselves in to authorities and soon found less revolutionary careers. More of the discontented attempted less violent escapes. In 1973 it was observed that many of the young had in recent years taken to the road like modern gypsies: "Spartanly dressed youth with outstretched thumbs or 'hippie vans' have become as common a sight on American highways as the cloverleaf exchange."[1] Some chose the traditional American road of escape to the frontier. By the mid-1970s, for instance, hundreds of radicals and hippies had settled in the rugged mountain country of Colorado, Montana, or elsewhere in the West, either in rundown mining towns or in isolated cabins far from the beaten path. Most of the new frontiersmen were not especially violent, though at least one, the "Unabomber," was to carry his private war against modern society into the 1990s by sending bombs through the mail. So many hippies settled in the isolated rural regions of northern California that in the 1980s the marijuana produced there was said to have become the state's largest single cash crop. As late as the mid-1980s, thousands gathered at the Rainbow Family Peace Gathering held each Fourth of July since 1972.[2]

More than a few tried to find independence on the land in the more isolated areas of the Northeast. In the early 1970s, Ray Mungo and a few other radicals established Total Loss Farm in Vermont with the aim of making peace with society on their terms. For a time, they achieved some success, although it was less in farming than in publishing various works about farm life with such titles as *The Food Garden* and *Living on the Earth*. This new version of the old Jeffersonian dream helped give *The Mother Earth News*, which billed itself as the "original country magazine," a circulation of over 800,000 well into the 1980s.

Many of the young sought refuge in exotic religion, joining a variety of cults where they hoped to find the peace and the enlightenment they had once sought through psychedelic drugs: Zen Buddhism, Taoism, Krishna consciousness, Sufism, transcendental meditation, Scientology, Jewish mysticism, Christian fundamentalism, Jews for Jesus—virtually any religion and belief not associated with the hated Establishment, including the wilder outlands of Satanism and witchcraft. Perhaps as many as a million young Americans joined one or more of the some 200 religious cults that sprang up in the 1970s. In place of political movements, de-

clared one observer, "gurus, swamis, roshis, dervishes, gods, and thera-
pists are building impressive movements and extensive institutions."[3]

Rennie Davis, an SDS leader, was a prominent convert to the Divine
Light Mission headed by a fifteen-year-old guru, Maharanji Ji. In 1973,
Davis reported that there were 150 Divine Light "centers" linked by Telex
machines and WATS lines, all working to convert his generation to the
new spirituality and, thus, to achieve the revolution that he had tried to
effect in the streets during the 1960s. Thousands of young people joined
Sun Myung Moon's Unification Church, whose president was a forties
baby, Neil Salonen; others tried the Society for Krishna Consciousness.
Such exotics generally offered the comfort of a "family" with a structured
life and a directing father far removed from the families and fathers the
converts had known as children. Later, many pursued their quest for something transcendent in the New Age movement, a mix of Asian religion,
occult and primitive spiritual beliefs, alternative medicine, and radical
environmentalism. In the 1980s, subscriptions to the *New Age Journal*,
founded in 1974, increased by 900 percent, and by one estimate there
were more than 11 million New Agers.

By requiring that their followers give up any drug habits, these faiths
often helped pave the way for a return home, although many of those
who returned brought with them at least some of their 1960s hopes and
resentments. Writing in the 1980s of her peers, Annie Gottlieb said there
was "something a little off" in their lives: "There seem to be a lot of
carpenters with college degrees and lawyers homesick for the Himalayas."[4]

Even when they did return to mainstream society, a great many dissenters refused to return to the religion of their childhood. Well-meaning
middle-class Protestantism was hardest hit by these defections. Main-line
churches such as the Methodists experienced the greatest losses, whereas
fundamentalist churches, like the cults, often attracted young converts
and for the same reason: they supplied clear answers to spiritual ques-
tions, while the established churches seemed to offer only good inten-
tions. In the late 1980s a poll of over 1,500 baby boomers revealed that
as children, 96 percent had been brought up in churchgoing households—
a reflection of the religious revival of the 1950s. As young adults, however, the majority had dropped out of organized religion for two years or
more. By 1990, many of these dropouts, especially the more conservative
ones, had returned to organized religion, but more than one-third had not.

In similar ways, political dissenters came home to established politics, reluctantly abandoning the fashionable hope of the late 1960s for

revolution. Attempting to find their way back on their own terms, they often tried to combine their occupations with continued efforts to change society, following the lead of Carl Oglesby, the former SDS leader who held a full-time job at IBM while continuing his political efforts on the weekends. One dissenter joined Cesar Chávez's farm workers' union; another, as a lawyer for a steel company, specialized in civil rights and environmental matters. Bernadine Dohrn, who had gone underground with other Weathermen but surfaced in the 1980s, eventually became an advocate for children's rights. In 1989 a survey of 212 participants in the Mississippi freedom summer of 1964 revealed that the great majority of them remained involved in reform causes.

For a time in the 1970s, political radicals achieved some influence in selected enclaves. In Berkeley, they elected several members of the city council, and in Madison, Wisconsin, they made Paul Soglin, a twenty-seven-year-old radical and former student, the mayor of the city. Sam Brown, the organizer of the 1968 McCarthy youth movement, was elected state treasurer of Colorado and attempted to use the office to find ways of serving the interests of the poor. In the summer of 1975, Brown, Soglin, and some 200 other radically inclined officials met at Madison for a Conference of Alternative State and Local Public Policies to devise ways by which they could work for fundamental change. They expressed a continued devotion to the ideal of participatory democracy, hoping that they could build a grassroots movement that would eventually mount an effective challenge to the Establishment.

The most prominent political effort was made by Tom Hayden in California. In the early 1970s, as he later recalled, Hayden had become convinced that the New Left, like the Old, had dwindled into a small, inbound, isolated enclave where "language turned to jargon, disputes were elevated to doctrinal heights, paranoia replaced openness, and the struggle to change each other became a substitute for changing the world." He resolved to return to society and politics—with some success. In 1976 he ran for the United States Senate and polled over a million votes in a losing cause. Although much of this substantial support came from both a strong anti-incumbent trend in the state and the appeal of his then wife and most prominent supporter, the actress Jane Fonda, Hayden believed his showing demonstrated that, as he said in another context, "the radicalism of the 1960s is fast becoming the common sense of the 1970s." In 1977 he and other largely California activists founded the Campaign for Economic Democracy to promote popular support for a wide-ranging radical program headed by an "Economic Bill of Rights which recognizes that every citizen is assured the right to work, health, housing, education, personal safety and environmental sanity."[5]

Soon after Hayden proclaimed this movement in his book *The American Future* (1980), however, the nation decided that it wanted a different future by electing Ronald Reagan, the hard-line enemy of California radicalism, as its next president. By this time, the entire baby-boom generation had reached voting age. Reagan, running on a platform hostile to government and to taxes, won more support (nearly 60 percent) from voters eighteen to thirty-nine than from those over forty. Two years later, Hayden was able to win a seat in the California state assembly, but that success came chiefly from his own and his wife's personal popularity and from a lavishly financed campaign. A decade later, long after he and Fonda were divorced, he won the Democratic nomination for mayor of Los Angeles but lost the election by a large majority.

It was not a time for radical idealism. In 1984, the year in which Reagan won a landslide reelection, only 41 percent of baby boomers identified themselves as liberals, far less than the two-thirds who had done so in the early 1970s. Much of their earlier liberalism had been a reflection of their radical disillusionment with government in the late 1960s, especially regarding the draft and Vietnam. Although the majority of democracy's children continued their opposition to racial and sexual discrimination in the 1980s, they did not share the old liberal faith in government, and many deserted the Democratic Party, some to vote Republican and others not to vote at all.

A few of the more fortunate radicals did find places where they could exert some longtime influence. Some editors of the underground press, benefiting from their experience in journalism, continued their criticisms of society in alternative papers such as the *Lansing Star*, which survived the collapse of the radical press movement, or from podiums on radio and in the schools. Peter Jensen of the *Eugene (Oregon) Augur* and Steve Abbott of the *Columbus (Ohio) Free Press* became instructors at nearby community colleges. Others, like former Weatherman Bill Ayres, equipped themselves with Ph.D.s and found places in university humanities and social science departments, where they attempted to make their disciplines serve the cause of radical change; there they helped create what critics came to denounce as "political correctness" in academia. By the late 1980s, Mark Rudd, who had spent seven years in hiding for his extremism, had found a job teaching in a school in New Mexico. At their worst, they substantiated conservative fears that they upheld an adversary culture hostile to society. At their best, they sustained the democratic ideal; numerous young historians, for instance, helped democratize the past by revealing the lives of the common people in ways that earlier generations of scholars had ignored.

Whereas the generally college-educated political radicals tended to find jobs in politics, academia, or social services, cultural rebels generally lacked the experience and the credentials for such work and had to look elsewhere. Many sought a future in their own small businesses, drawing on the counterculture to become independent craftsmen, printers and publishers, and especially retailers. Bakeries, microbreweries, wineries, health food stores, organic gardens, food cooperatives, head shops, and other exotic ventures greatly expanded the freedom of choice among consumers, offering products and services not available in the corporate world. In the process, they changed the dietary and spending habits of society. Ray Mungo, a founder of the Liberation News organization, declared in his 1979 book *Cosmic Profit* that "the marketplace is rife with products that we consumers never could have imagined a few years ago. There's big money in natural foods, natural soaps, weird footwear, metaphysical notions, new games, . . . new magazines and newspapers catering to special interests that scarcely existed before, recreational equipment, arts and crafts, cottage industries and many more."[6] Ironically, the counterculture served to expand the democratic choices of the consumer-oriented economy that it opposed.

At least a few baby boomers such as Jerry Rubin, by the 1980s a Wall Street entrepreneur, were willing to come to terms with the business establishment. In the corporate world the number of managers aged twenty-four to thirty-four increased by 110 percent between 1970 and 1980, nearly twice the growth of that age group generally. The 1980s saw the much publicized rise of the "Yuppies," or young urban professionals: the estimated 4 million Americans between twenty-five and thirty-nine who had incomes of more than $40,000 a year, a large sum for the times. One observer concluded that their success derived less from hard work than from skill in "networking"—creating supportive relationships with like-minded, like-aged people—often using skills developed during the days of youth protests.

Many other young job seekers, however, were hostile to accepting any place within the hated Establishment and tried to avoid it by taking low-wage jobs, often with the greatest resentment. The early 1970s saw rising doubts about the willingness of young adults to fit into the workaday economy. Drugs, the rip-off morality of the Yippies, the counterculture rejection of the work ethic, the emphasis on self-satisfaction, and habits of protest seemed to lead some rebels to take out their resentment of authority within the industrial system. At the new General Motors automobile plant in Lordstown, Ohio, for example, young workers expressed their dissatisfaction by sabotaging production. The magazine *Liberation* published a long poem, "Lordstown," which depicted the plant as one example of an inhuman industrial mechanism and declared ominously: "There are plots being hatched in the bathrooms / & crosshairs etched in the necks of foremen in a thousand Lordstowns."[7]

The threat was much exaggerated, but undoubtedly such dissatisfaction adversely affected American industry at a time of growing competition in the emerging global economy. By the mid-1970s, owing to many factors, industrial stagnation had come to replace the prosperous and easy employment days in which the forties generation had grown up. Near the end of 1974 a writer in *Ramparts* declared that the coming December would be "the last Christmas in America."[8] The future was not quite that bad, but between 1973 and 1980 the median income of young men did fall by an estimated 17 percent. And in 1988 a survey conducted by *Rolling Stone* indicated that the forties generation had some special problems with downward mobility: more than 40 percent of those polled between ages thirty-five and forty-five doubted that they would be as well off as their parents.

Whatever road they took, however, by the end of the 1980s the vast majority of those born in the 1940s had found places in conventional society, acquired homes and families, and accepted things as they were. As early as 1977, Morris Dickstein noted that the sixties emphasis on self-expression and self-development had given way to a more constricted vision in which often simply getting by was enough, and that tendency continued to grow as the enthusiasm of the 1960s became an ever more distant memory. It was a trend bolstered by the greater conservatism of the second-wave baby boomers. In 1987, Fred Siegel warned Democrats not to count on support from the young: "Today, boomers are divided between those born before 1954, who are on the whole distinctive in their criticisms of American institutions, and those born after 1954, who are more like the rest of the population."[9] The disastrous Democratic defeat in the 1988 presidential elections soon confirmed Siegel's judgment.

A few hopes for a revival of sixties radicalism survived. In the late 1980s, Richard Flacks declared that "cultural pockets" existed in the United States which would assure the transmission of the left tradition to the next generation, animating future change.[10] And the authors of *Where Have All the Flowers Gone?* (1989) saw the beginnings of a counterculture revival that they hoped would have a significant influence on the 1990s. At nearly the same time, sociologist Bennett M. Berger noted that elements of both political and cultural radicalism were in the process of incorporating themselves into established society, including American conservatism, and so were likely to survive even the demise of the old liberalism.

Thinkers like Flacks and Berger found support for their hopes in the recognition that the sixties movement had deep roots in the past. And so it did. In historical perspective, democracy's children were a special breed with a special purpose. Looking back from the 1980s, Annie Gottlieb called those born between 1944 and 1949 the "epicenter of a cultural earthquake."[11] They and others of the forties generation were part of a grand old tradition that extended backward in time through the left liberalism of the New Deal to even earlier efforts to realize the American promise of "life, liberty, and the pursuit of happiness" for all. From early childhood through their school years in the decade after World War II, they had been educated both to a high regard for themselves as individuals and to the fundamental importance of democratic ideals, and with the civil rights movement of the early 1960s they were able to celebrate their advance into adulthood by participating in the great struggle to overthrow a great denial of that promise.

The triumph over racial discrimination was a major step forward in the history of American democracy and the fulfillment of much of the mission of the new generation. Eventually, democracy's children expanded the American promise—in ways often not anticipated—to include women, gays, the transgendered, and other previously excluded groups into a radical new social ideal: a society where the great and not yet fully disclosed diversity of the human race would be free to develop all its unique qualities in a world of peace and harmony. Except in earlier utopian forms, that ideal was truly new.

These triumphs were both disrupted and enriched by two profound developments of the sixties. One was the eruption of the counterculture movement, which deepened as well as complicated the efforts to change society by pushing the ideal of self-realization in new and sometimes outrageous directions. In every generation of the young there had been rebels, but the sheer size of the baby-boom generation gave rebellion a critical mass that seemed capable of transforming society. Despite its demands for cultural revolution, this movement was basically benign. If it was rebellion against established values and tastes, it was a gentle rebellion in the name of peace and love—though it was an ineffectual rebellion, destined to be absorbed into mass popular culture.

There was no peace and love, however, in the second development, the intrusion of the war in Vietnam. Democracy's children, born in the era of a "good war," now had to confront the menace of what they came increasingly to see as a bad war, a denial of democracy at home and abroad. Although only a minority of them were actually compelled to serve in Vietnam, they abhorred the idea of being coerced into a bloody and futile conflict. The civil rights movement had encountered brutality, especially in the South, that had generated fear and hatred among the young, but nothing comparable to the effects of the Vietnam War and the events surrounding it. It was a nightmare entry into maturity for those born in the 1940s, a profound shock that brought bitterness and despair, turning many of the young against government, against society, and often against the liberalism that had done so much to shape their ideals.

A special generation in its positive destiny had become special in its anger and depression. Sometimes it was identified with the special word "love," but love as word and deed had certainly been a familiar part of earlier generations. More nearly unique, and more revealing of those whose idealism turned into a sour skepticism regarding authority, was the word— probably their greatest contribution to the English language—they so often repeated and shouted: "Bullshit!" It was the shibboleth of a generation educated to democratic hopes and then shocked, by the realities and complexities of the world that confronted them, into rage and cynicism.

The great scar left by the Vietnam War was to have a significant effect on that generation in the 1970s as it reached the next stage of maturity, that of family and parenthood. Its deviation from the norm here would have a long-term influence on a future not yet realized, forming an interesting epilogue to the disturbing history of democracy's children.

NOTES

1. *New York Times* (July 12, 1970): VI:6, 39; *Rolling Stone* (January 3, 1974): 50–51.

2. Ivan Goldman, "New Hermits of the Rockies," *The Nation* (September 20, 1975): 50–51.

3. Andrew Kopkind, "Mystic Politics," *Ramparts* (July 1973): 24–26.

4. Gottlieb, *Do You Believe in Magic?* 105–6, 113.

5. Dan Blackburn, "The Hayden-Tunny Bout," *The Nation* (August 2, 1975): 44–45; Tom Hayden, *The American Future* (Boston, 1980), 3–4, 303–10.

6. Mungo, *Cosmic Profit*, xiv, xx, 96.

7. *Liberation* (April 1972): 24–25.

8. Terence McCarthy, "The Last Christmas in America," *Ramparts* (December 1974–75): 49–64.

9. Fred Siegel, "Baby Boomerang: Why the Democrats Can't Count on Generational Politics," *Commonweal* (August 14, 1987): 442–45.

10. Richard Flacks, *Making History: The American Left and the American Mind* (New York, 1988), 285–86.

11. Gottlieb, *Do You Believe in Magic?* 10.

Epilogue: Baby Bust and Beyond

Modern demographic history returned to normal with a vengeance in the 1970s. It was no surprise that in the later 1960s the birthrate in America began to fall, since the high fertility of the baby boom had been abnormal, the exception to the modern trend of diminished procreation. What *was* surprising was the extent of the fall in the 1970s rate. At the end of the sixties the Census Bureau predicted a rate of no fewer than eighty-four births per thousand. In fact, in 1973 the rate dropped to sixty-nine and fell even lower the next year. Because of the growing number of potential mothers—those born in the first half of the baby boom—demographers predicted an increase in the actual number of births during this period even as the rate declined; instead, the number of annual births in the 1970s fell below the level required to replace the parent population. "We are now experiencing," said Paul Woodring in 1974, "the most rapid decline in birthrate in the nation's history."[1] The late 1970s brought a modest upswing in the number of births (the result of there being more potential mothers) but no reversal of the overall downward trend in the birthrate.

One evident explanation was improvement in the technology of birth control, especially the birth control pill and such devices as the IUD; by 1969, about one of every five women of childbearing age was "on the Pill." Less evident were the reasons for actually using the technology. In some part, they arose from environmental concerns over the effects on the Earth of rapid population growth. Although such concerns had been expressed after World War II, they had not been strong enough to dampen the baby boom. They grew more serious in the sixties, in part because of the anticipated effects of the baby boom itself on available natural resources. At the beginning of the decade, one demographer warned that the nation's "irresponsible birthrate" would produce one billion Americans by the year 2060, a threat to the entire Earth, since Americans were already consuming, by one estimate, one-half of the world's nonrenewable resources.[2] In 1969 a presidential study commission reported that the majority of Americans had already decided that birth control was necessary, and this opinion was confirmed by a Gallup poll in which more than two-thirds of young adults agreed with the assertion that continuous population growth would be detrimental to "the quality of your life and your family."[3]

Idealism was certainly a factor in this baby bust, but such things as environmental pieties took second place to the personal ambitions of the maturing Me Generation. The best-educated generation in American history expected to reap the financial rewards of its education, and one of the most tormented generations expected to find the satisfactions it believed had been denied it. Such ambitions left little room for the restraints and responsibilities of parenthood, especially when it became evident that the flood of new job seekers into a stagnating economy was making success difficult. These economic concerns were reinforced by the social resentments and desperate feelings raised by the war in Vietnam. Where World War II, the good war, had induced optimism regarding the future, Lyndon Johnson's war generated strong negative feelings, which diminished thoughts of having families and often led to deferred parenthood or none at all. A 1960 Gallup poll indicated that 45 percent of those polled would prefer four or more children; in 1971, only 23 percent even dreamed of so large a family. A decade later, polls revealed that baby boomers born in the 1940s and early 1950s were far more likely than other groups to agree with the statement, "It would be unfair to bring a child into the world," and a survey of those from this generation who had been involved in the civil rights movement indicated that they were especially inclined not to want children.[4]

The disposition against procreation was especially strong among college-educated women, a not unexpected but notably different view from the attitudes of such women in the 1940s. Completing a degree became a common goal among young women, and by the 1970s, their ambition to climb the ladder of career success was often strengthened by a feminist determination to open the way for women in general; idealism thus strengthened self-interest and led to decisions to defer, if not to forgo, marriage. In 1986 the median age of women when they married rose to a level unmatched since early in the century, reducing the number of childbearing years.

Not surprisingly, women between twenty and twenty-four had some 40 percent fewer children in 1969 than that age group had had in 1960. And the chances of later recovery from the decline were diminished by other factors opposing procreation among Americans generally. By 1983 the percentage of women ages twenty-five to thirty-four who worked outside the home was double that of 1960; the percentage of women ages twenty to thirty-four—the years of greatest fertility for adult women—who were single increased by 50 percent, and the proportion who were divorced more than tripled.

Once this process started, it tended, like the baby boom, to be self-reinforcing. Having few or no children became fashionable, sanctioned by the currently popular philosophy of zero population growth. In the 1970s an estimated 10 million Americans had themselves sterilized to avoid having children. In the early 1970s the fertility rate fell below the minimum believed necessary to replace the existing population over time (2.1 children per woman of childbearing age) and remained below the replacement level into the 1980s, threatening to produce a baby bust at least as long as the two decades of the baby boom. By 1986, when the birthrate reached 65 per thousand, the lowest in American history, the childbearing years of women in the first wave of the baby-boom—women between thirty-four and forty-three—were rapidly vanishing.

It was at this time that Annie Gottlieb took note of her four closest women friends from the sixties and realized that though two were childless, the other two had "married younger men at the eleventh hour to have babies."[5] Such an eleventh-hour decision in favor of motherhood was common enough to bring an upward swing in the late 1980s in the number of births, which by 1989 exceeded 4 million, a number unequaled since the peak years of the baby boom. The cause, however, was the increase in the number of women of childbearing age to 54 million, the largest number in American history. The general birthrate, in contrast, remained below the replacement level.

The baby bust had numerous significant effects. Between 1970 and 1977, for instance, elementary school enrollments declined by close to 5 million pupils, forcing cutbacks in the first level of public education to have earlier experienced the effects of the baby boom. Soon, the shrinkage reached the high schools and then the colleges, requiring adjustments in their overextended staffs and overbuilt plants. Eventually, some Americans began to ponder the consequences of this birth reversal for the future. Much of the concern focused on the time when the aging baby boomers would begin to retire. Having failed to reproduce themselves, they had also failed to provide a younger generation large enough to support their retirement without sacrifice on someone's part. By the 2020s, when the last of the boomers would reach age 65, the ratio of workers to retirees was expected to fall from over 3 to 1 to less than 2 to 1. As most of the now aging boomers expected to live about as well in retirement as they did during their working life, it was evident that they would take a large share of the wealth produced by younger Americans. By one estimate, their retirement was likely to engross 45 percent (by another, it was 65 percent!) of the entire federal budget by 2030 unless changes were made in the national retirement system.

Prior to the 1990s, few observers pondered the larger consequences of the baby bust, but in 1987, Ben J. Wattenberg, a popular expert on demographics, warned that "the birth dearth" threatened the future of the United States and other Western nations. He believed that the decline of the white European population relative to burgeoning Third World populations would have a serious destabilizing effect throughout the world. Something similar would occur in the United States with the relative shrinkage of the white middle class, in which the birth dearth was most evident. Besides this decline of white European culture, Wattenberg predicted that the aging of the American population (the median age was expected to reach forty-five by 2050) would bring a significant lessening of vitality and creativity. He warned that unless something were done quickly to increase the birthrate, the United States and the West in general were headed for an irreversible decline, "a Modern tragedy." To prevent that tragedy, he proposed that the national government make bonus grants of $2,000 a year for each new child, but he concluded that it would take more than money to reverse the situation: "If our young people remain a generation that can be characterized as 'me-oriented' or 'self-actualizing,' they probably will continue to have few babies. But suppose we reinvigorate this generation to understand and take pride in the fact that they are part of a remarkable, potent, productive, human beneficent culture. Suppose our young come to know in the marrow of their bones that the West . . . is the last best hope of mankind."[6]

Critics did not respond well to Wattenberg's argument, some dismissing it as nothing more than a new version of the old racist concern over the "yellow peril." Even if it were a valid lesson, it would not be easily learned by a generation whose spokespersons had grown to adulthood persuaded of the corruptness of their modern society. They had been called an idealistic generation—which they had often been—but their most enduring attitude seems to have been cynicism and suspicion regarding public authority and the public good. Although that cynicism was not infrequently mated with a commitment to protecting the future environment, it hardly inclined people to accept appeals to preserve the future of Western civilization.

In their early conditioning in the 1940s and 1950s, democracy's children had acquired a commitment to work to expand justice and self-government for all, and they were in significant respects successful in carrying out their mission. In the process, though, they had exhausted much of the nation's stock of ideals in their 1960s war against the System; a generation so often hailed for its idealism bequeathed to the future a much weakened idealism. It was not surprising, then, that a generation so often portrayed as hostile to the supposed materialistic values of their parents should help forge a highly successful economy in the 1990s, where materialistic values prevailed.

The world economic boom of the 1990s promised to lessen the extent of the retirement problem, and America's lenient immigration policies provided replacements for much of the missing native labor resulting from the birth dearth. In the twenty-first century, it is possible that the largest generation in American history may be able to retire to the affluence it had known as children—beneficiaries of the very modernity that many had learned to condemn. Possibly, their last-minute demand for health care and for wheelchairs and coffins can stimulate the economy as their childhood demands did. However, the economic stagnation of the first years of the new century challenges hopes for the future.

Will the nation under the influence of this aging population be able to recover the vitality of its spirit and ideals, the vitality of its youth? The years surrounding the advent of the new millennium have had their idealistic moments, but their most notable characteristic has been an infatuation with dollars rather than doctrines, with spending rather than contributing. As democracy's children move on through time toward their eventual disappearance, dreams of immortality appear. When he was asked what he would want as his epitaph, the veteran radical journalist Paul Krassner reached back to his early days in the 1950s as an editor of *Mad* magazine to provide an answer: "IF I WERE MADE OF STYROFOAM, I WOULD STILL BE AROUND."[7] It is fortunate for the future that this creative but also troubling generation was made of the same material as humans in general.

NOTES

1. Paul Woodring, "Our Unpredictable Birthrate," *Saturday Review* (March 9, 1974): 6.
2. Lincoln Day, "Our Irresponsible Birthrate," *Reader's Digest* (November 1960): 75–78.

3. Bremner et al., *Children and Youth*, 3:957, 963.

4. Geoge H. Gallup, *The Gallup Polls: Public Opinion, 1935–1971* (New York: Random House, 1972), 3:2299; Siegel, "Baby-Boomerang," 445.

5. Gottlieb, *Do You Believe in Magic?* 4.

6. "The Birth Dearth," *U.S. News* (June 22, 1987): 56–58.

7. Quoted in Chepesuik, *Sixties Radicals*, 40.

Bibliographical Essay

There is a great range of materials available on the baby-boom generation, including those born in the 1940s. Landon Y. Jones, *Great Expectations: America and the Baby-Boom Generation* (New York: Coward, McCann & Geoghegan, 1980), remains the benchmark for such studies, although it is weakened by a failure to recognize sufficently the differences between those born in the 1940s and those in the 1950s. For a general overview of the United States during the period in which the forties generation was shaped, see Geoffrey Perret, *A Dream of Greatness: The American People, 1945–1963* (New York: Coward, McCann & Geoghegan, 1979). For public opinion surveys during these years, there is nothing better than George H. Gallup, *The Gallup Polls: Public Opinion, 1935–1971*, 3 vols. (New York: Random House, 1972). Popular magazines are important both as reflections of prevailing attitudes and as influences in creating those attitudes, the most significant here being *Atlantic Monthly, Reader's Digest*, and *Saturday Evening Post*.

Important insights regarding the rearing and education of the children of the period can be found in the significant collection of documents by Robert H. Bremner et al., *Children and Youth in America* (Cambridge, MA: Harvard University Press, 1974), especially volume 3, and in two primary influences: Benjamin Spock, *Baby and Child Care*, a popular guidebook for parents that went through several editions; and *Parents Magazine*, a major influence in the 1950s. Other sources of special importance are Mary Cable, *The Little Darlings: A History of Child Rearing in America* (New York: Charles Scribner's Sons, 1975); Oscar and Mary F. Handlin, *Facing Life: Youth and Family in American History* (Boston: Little, Brown, 1971); Susan M. Hartman, *The Home Front and Beyond: American Women in the 1940s* (Boston: Twayne, 1982); Elaine Tyler May, *Homeward Bound: American Families in the Cold War Era* (New York: Basic Books, 1988); and Margaret Mead and Martha Wolfenstein, *Childhood in Contemporary Cultures* (Chicago: University of Chicago Press, 1955). For education, see especially James B. Conant, *The American High*

School Today (New York: McGraw-Hill, 1959); Lawrence Cremin, *The Transformation of the School: Progressivism in American Education, 1876–1957* (New York: Random House, 1964); I. L. Kandel's insightful *The New Era of Education* (Boston: Houghton Mifflin, 1955); C. Winfield Scott et al., eds., *The Great Debate: Our Schools in Crisis* (Englewood Cliffs, NJ: Prentice-Hall, 1959); and the magazine *School and Society*.

The troubled world of adolescence evoked numerous interesting books, most notably Paul Goodman's very influential *Growing Up Absurd* (New York: Vintage Books, 1960), and his *Compulsory Miseducation* (New York: Horizon Press, 1964). Useful for understanding important concerns about juvenile delinquency in the late 1950s are Edgar Z. Friedenberg, *The Vanishing Adolescent*, 2d ed. (Boston: Beacon Press, 1964); and Harrison Salisbury, *The Shook-Up Generation* (New York: Harper & Brothers, 1958).

Higher education provided a tumultuous doorway into American society for the forties generation, as the following books on the subject indicate: Carnegie Commision on Higher Education, *Reform on Campus* (New York: McGraw-Hill, 1972); Allen Cartter, *Higher Education in the United States* (Washington, DC: American Council on Education, 1964); Christopher Jencks and David Riesman, *The Academic Revolution* (Garden City, NY: Doubleday, 1968); Clark Kerr, *The Uses of the University* (Cambridge, MA: Harvard University Press, 1972); Robert S. Morison, ed., *The Contemporary University* (Boston: Houghton Mifflin, 1966); and David Riesman, *On Higher Education* (San Francisco: Jossey-Bass, 1981).

On the student response to higher education, see Seymour Martin Lipset and Gerald M. Schaflander, *Passion and Politics: Student Activism in America* (Boston: Little, Brown, 1971); David Mallery, *Ferment on Campus* (New York: Harper & Row, 1966); Robert Nisbet, *The Degradation of the Academic Dogma* (New York: Basic Books, 1971); and Edward E. Sampson, ed., *Stirrings out of Apathy: Student Activism and the Decade of Protest*, special issue, *Journal of Social Issues* 23, no. 3 (1967).

There are numerous books dealing with African Americans starting with the works of the black sociologist E. Franklin Frazier, particularly his classic *Black Bourgeoisie* (New York: Free Press, 1957) and *Negro Youth at the Crossways* (New York, 1967). Also see Jesse Bernard, *Marriage and Family among Negroes* (Englewood Cliffs, NJ: Prentice-Hall, 1966); Joe R. Feagan and Harlan Hahn, *Ghetto Riots* (New York: Macmillan, 1973); David R. Goldfield and James E. Lane, eds., *The Enduring Ghetto* (Philadelphia: J. B. Lippincott, 1973); Mary Ellen Goodman, *Race Awareness in Young Children* (Cambridge, MA: Addison-Wesley,

1952); and Gilbert Osofsky's valuable *The Burden of Race* (New York: Harper & Row, 1967). The *Journal of Negro Education* provides numerous articles on black child development as well as education.

For the African American civil rights protest movement, see the documentary collection edited by Francis Broderick and August Meier, *Negro Protest Thought in the Twentieth Century* (Indianapolis: Bobbs-Merrill, 1965); Stokely Carmichael and Charles V. Hamilton, *Black Power* (New York: Vintage Books, 1967); and Louis E. Lomax, *The Negro Revolt* (New York: New American Library, 1963). See also James McEvoy and Abraham Miller, eds., *Black Power and Student Rebellion* (Belmont, CA: Wadsworth, 1969); Charles E. Silberman, *Crisis in Black and White* (New York: Random House, 1964); and Howard Zinn, *SNCC: The New Abolitionists* (Boston: Beacon Press, 1965).

The emergence of the New Left and student radicalism has been amply documented in, among others, Geoff Andrews et al., eds., *New Left, New Right and Beyond: Taking the Sixties Seriously* (New York: St. Martin's Press, 1999); Edward J. Bacciocco Jr., *The New Left in America* (Stanford, CA: Hoover Institution, 1974); Mitchell Cohen and Dennis Hale, *The New Student Left* (Boston: Beacon Hill, 1965); Hale Draper, *Berkeley: The New Student Revolt* (New York: Grove Press, 1965); Richard Flacks, *Making History: The American Left and the American Mind* (New York: Columbia University Press, 1988); Maurice Isserman, *If I Had a Hammer: The Death of the Old Left and the Birth of the New Left* (New York: Basic Books, 1987); Seymour Martin Lipset and Sheldon Wolin, eds., *The Berkeley Student Revolt* (Garden City, NY: Doubleday, 1965); Carl Oglesby, *New Left Reader* (New York: Grove Press, 1969); and James Weinstein and David W. Eakins, eds., *For a New America: Essay in History and Politics from Studies on the Left, 1959–1967* (New York: Random House, 1970).

Good studies of the 1960s, especially as they relate to youth, include Terry Anderson, *The Movement of the Sixties* (New York: Oxford University Press, 1995); Todd Gitlin's excellent *The Sixties* (New York: Bantam Books, 1987); Maurice Isserman and Michael Kazin, *America Divided: The Civil War of the 1960s* (New York: Oxford University Press, 2000); Peter Joseph, ed., *Good Times: An Oral History of America in the Nineteen Sixties* (New York: Charterhouse, 1973); James Miller, *Democracy Is in the Streets: From Port Huron to the Siege of Chicago* (New York: Simon & Schuster, 1987); Sohnya Sayres et al., eds., *The 60s without Apology* (Minneapolis: University of Minnesota Press, 1984); David Steigerwald, *The Sixties and the End of Modern America* (New York: St.

Martin's Press, 1995); and Milton Viorst, *Fire in the Streets: America in the 1960s* (New York: Simon & Schuster, 1979).

   For the period of the Vietnam War, the following are especially useful: Lawrence M. Baskir and William A. Strauss, *Chance and Circumstance: The Draft, the War, and the Vietnam Generation* (New York: Alfred A. Knopf, 1978); David Cortright's devastating portrait, *Soldiers in Revolt: The American Military Today* (Garden City, NY: Doubleday, 1975); Kenneth J. Heinman, *Campus Wars: The Peace Movement at American Universities in the Vietnam Era* (New York: New York University Press, 1993); Tom Hayden, *Rebellion in Newark* (New York: Random House, 1967); Louis Menashe and Ronald Radosh, eds., *Teach-Ins U.S.A.* (New York: Praeger, 1967); Robert W. Mullen, *Blacks and Vietnam* (Washington, DC: University Press of America, 1981); and Nancy Zaroulis and Gerald Sullivan, *Who Spoke Up? American Protests against the War in Vietnam* (Garden City, NY: Doubleday, 1984. Also see two periodicals, *Liberation* and *Ramparts*.

   The counterculture movement of the 1960s excited much popular interest that produced, among other books, Anthony Casale and Philip Lerman, *Where Have All the Flowers Gone?* (Kansas City, MO: Andrews & McMead, 1989); Morris Dickstein, *Gates of Eden: American Culture in the Sixties* (New York: Basic Books, 1977); Robert J. Glessing, *The Underground Press in America* (Bloomington: Indiana University Press, 1970); Lawrence Lipton's study of the Beats, *The Holy Barbarians* (New York: Julian Mesner, 1959); William L. Partridge, *The Hippie Ghetto* (New York: Holt, Rinehart & Winston, 1973); Charles Reich, *The Greening of America* (New York: Random House, 1970); Theodore Roszak, *The Making of A Counterculture* (Garden City, NY: Doubleday, 1969); and *Time* Magazine, *The Hippies* (New York: Time, 1967).

   For the hippie communes of the period, see Richard Fairfield, *Communes USA* (Baltimore, MD: Penguin Books, 1972); and Oliver Popenoe and Cris Popenoe, *Seeds of Tomorrow* (San Francisco: Harper & Row, 1984). On drugs, see Martin A. Lee and Bruce Sclain, *Acid Dreams: The CIA, LSD, and the Sixties Rebellion* (New York, 1985); and Timothy Leary, "In the Beginning," *Esquire* (July 1968): 83–87, 116–17. For music, see Arnold Shaw, *The Rock Revolution* (London, 1969). For the Yippies, see Abbie Hoffman, *Revolution for the Hell of It* (New York: Dial Press, 1968); and Jerry Rubin, *Growing [Up] at Thirty-Seven* (New York: M. Evans, 1976).

   The effort to change society broke into fragments in the 1970s. Among numerous interesting books for this period are Ron Chepesuik, *Sixties,*

Then and Now (Jefferson, NC: McFarland & Co., 1995); John D'Emilio, *Sexual Politics, Sexual Communities: The Making of a Homosexual Minority in the United States* (Chicago: University of Chicago Press, 1983); Thomas Ferguson and Joel Rogers, *Right Turn: The Decline of the Democrats and the Future of American Politics* (New York: Hill & Wang, 1986); Paul Gottfried and Thomas Fleming, *The Conservative Movement* (Boston: Twayne, 1988); Tom Hayden, *The American Future* (Boston: South End Press, 1980); Roger Kimball, *Tenured Radicals* (New York, 1990); Peter H. Lindert, *Fertility and Scarcity in America* (Princeton: Princeton University Press, 1978); Meredith Maran, *What It's Like to Live Now* (New York: Bantam Books, 1995); Michael Nova and Robert Dawidoff, *Created Equal: Why Gay Rights Matter in America* (New York: St. Martin's Press, 1994); Wade C. Roof, *A Generation of Seekers* (San Francisco, 1993); John J. Talamini, *Boys Will Be Girls: The Hidden World of the Heterosexual Male Transvestite* (Lanham, MD: University Press of America, 1982); Leslie A. Westoff and Charles Westoff, *From Now to Zero* (Boston: Little, Brown, 1971); Nancy Whittier, *Feminist Generations* (Philadelphia: Temple University Press, 1995); and Daniel Yankelovich, *The New Morality* (New York: McGraw-Hill, 1974).

Index